knock, knock

knock, knock

Shedding Light on Jehovah's
Witness at the Door

ruth baker

TATE PUBLISHING & *Enterprises*

Published by Tate Publishing & Enterprises, LLC
127 E. Trade Center Terrace | Mustang, Oklahoma 73064 USA
1.888.361.9473 | www.tatepublishing.com

Tate Publishing is committed to excellence in the publishing industry. The company reflects the philosophy established by the founders, based on Psalms 68:11,
"The Lord gave the word and great was the company of those who published it."

Book design copyright © 2007 by Tate Publishing, LLC. All rights reserved.
Cover design by Lindsay B. Behrens
Interior design by Leah LeFlore

Published in the United States of America

ISBN: 978-1-60247-565-6
1. Theology and Doctrine: Contemporary
07.07.27

Dedicated to

the memory of Mike Chilton

A true Son of God
who revealed to me what God can do in a life.
I pray that someone will see Jesus in me,
just as I saw Him in Mike.

Table of contents

Foreword

When someone leaves a cult, or a false religious system, what follows is frequently akin to moving alone to a foreign country. The longer the cult involvement has lasted, the more severe and devastating can be the loss that follows leaving it. It is not unusual that the severance leads to deep depression in the former member-even to suicide.

As an ex-Mormon, I remember feeling that I had been alienated from human society altogether, and that I could never, ever be restored to normalcy. Add to that years of brainwashing with false doctrines and hundreds of "rules" and the results are nothing less than horrific.

This is the reason that I rejoice when I come across another resource that a child of God can use in his/her attempt to "set the captives free" from cult involvement. And since the Christian's objective is never cult extraction alone, it is also a wonderful tool to bring the Jehovah's Witnesses (in this case) to Jesus Christ and His true and *only* Gospel! (Gal. 1:6–9)

In this book, Ruth Baker gives us a rare glimpse into the dangerous Watchtower organization. She exposes some of their most serious doctrinal errors, unbiblical teachings, cultic behaviors, and false prophecies, while, at the same time, she implores her Christian readers to reach out to the deluded Witnesses with the love and truth of Jesus Christ.

As an ex-cultist, I appreciate the fact that she has room to talk: she has "walked a mile in their moccasins," as the old Indian saying goes! It is very obvious, from reading just the first chapter, that she has a heartfelt calling in reaching her former brothers and sisters in the J.W. organization for Christ.

Unfortunately, the average Christian householders who open their doors to Mormons and Jehovah's Witnesses, have very little (if any at all) skills and knowledge in reaching them for Christ. Therefore, one of two things usually happen: they send the "door knockers" away un-evangelized, or they begin a series of cleverly twisted "discussions" with them, which often lead to future memberships in these un-Christian, but zealous groups! Both scenarios are tragic.

It is estimated that over 80% of all Mormon converts belonged to Christian denominations before they joined! The statistic is very parallel with the J.W.s. No Christian should feel unprepared in dealing with these two of the fastest growing religions in our land, especially when they are a literal mission field on our doorsteps!

It is my prayer that this book will help to change that for whoever reads and studies it. May it serve as another valuable tool for changing some "dead man walking" into a true witness for Christ, for all eternity!

In His grace,
Agusta Harting
Author, cult-counselor, ex-Mormon

Jesus and the forces
of darkness

You have probably had days when you were busy doing something at home and there came a knock at the front door. You weren't expecting anyone. Who could it be? You open the door, and to your dismay it is none other than Jehovah's Witnesses again! You probably had one of the same reactions that many others had. Maybe you told them you have your own beliefs and church and slowly shut the door. Perhaps you listened quietly and took their magazines, book, Bible, or tract just to get rid of them. Perhaps you engaged them in a discussion just to prove them wrong. Despite what your response might have been, the result of most visitations by Jehovah's Witnesses to your home, or anyone's home, was probably one of frustration, anger, or a determination to get out the heavy artillery for the next time they come. Come on now; you know it's true. But, perhaps you had another feeling entirely-wanting to make a defense of your faith but not knowing how.

I know how important it is for someone to give a defense

of his faith. I have been on both sides of the fence-so to speak. For twenty years I was the person standing on someone's doorstep ringing the door bell. Yes, I was a baptized, dedicated Jehovah's Witness. But I saw the light and am now a born-again child of God. I must say, however, that although I was filled with unspeakable joy and freedom, I was truly heartbroken because I couldn't understand why I had been in the darkness so long. I actually asked God, "Why didn't you show me how wrong I was before this? Why didn't someone say something that would have at least shed some light into my darkness? I could have done so much more for You when I was a young person." I wasn't placing the responsibility of my actions onto anyone else. I just didn't understand.

Nevertheless, I trusted in Him and received the strong conviction that someday in God's timing, everything I experienced would be turned into something good. I just didn't know what, who, when, how, or why. Then, all of these things progressively started to take shape.

Starting about a year ago, I had several Spirit-filled Christians say that they really had the desire to give a defense of their faith. Some would specifically say that they would like to give a defense of their faith to anyone who would ask them, but they didn't know how. I was able to help these people by sharing spiritual insights I have received and also send them books on basic Christian doctrines. Others would tell me that Jehovah's Witnesses would make a call at their home, but, although they tried numerous avenues to give a defense, nothing worked. In fact, one stated that a J.W. came up with something that shut him down completely. In other words, that person was unable to refute or explain what the Witness said. I was able to encourage and instruct them by exposing some of the Jehovah's Witnesses' teachings and methods. I might add here that these examples are not to throw negative reflection on any of these Christians. They faithfully attend and participate in their churches, as well as read and know their Bibles. Something else was going on here.

The awareness soon took hold that now I knew the "who" and part of the "what" of my purpose. I was to help strengthen, instruct, and equip Christians to give a proper defense of the Gospel. While I was grateful for the opportunity to be of whatever help I could, there still seemed to be something missing. Then, several months later I had another "revelation."

I was doing some task around the house that was totally unrelated in thought and deed to this project. All of the sudden, in a split second really, the Spirit came to me in a clear but small, still voice, "Do it now!" No, I wasn't hearing voices, but I absolutely had no doubt about what I was to do and when I was supposed to do it. It was something that had already been planted deep inside of me, but now it started to take roots. I was to put together an instruction manual on how to give a Christian defense to Jehovah's Witnesses. I now knew the who, what, when, and how. I still needed to know why.

I found out the "why" just a couple of weeks ago. I went to the official Watchtower Bible and Tract Society's website because I wanted to know the total number of currently dedicated Witnesses. I discovered this information, but more importantly I learned something that absolutely alarmed me. The Society's 2005 report states that there were more than 6.5 million baptized Witnesses worldwide in 235 countries. These witnesses conducted more than 6 million Bible studies while engaging in more than 1 billion ministry hours. I wasn't shocked about these numbers, but what I discovered next sent a shockwave through my soul and spirit. So much so that I was literally drawn closer to the computer screen because I couldn't believe what I saw. *There were more than 16 million people who attended their 2005 memorial services. This Memorial service is at its fundamental foundation, the same as Christian communion or the Lord's Supper with two exceptions: only members of the 144,000 partake of it, and it is celebrated only once a year on Nisan 14 of the Jewish calendar.* Only a person who has been associated with the Watchtower Society can recognize the significance of this number of people attending the memorial service: *Only people who have been well indoctrinated into Jehovah's Witness beliefs attend this service. It means that more than 10 million of these attendees have not been baptized,* yet. *But, it is abundantly clear that millions are close to becoming full-fledged members in a short time!* Folks, here is the bottom line: the more Witnesses there are, the more people will receive visits from them. Now, we all now the 'why; we must get prepared for our defense of the Gospel and now. I have told you all these things because it brings us face to face with several very important facts that all Christians must be aware of.

First and foremost, we have to recognize that all Christians are in a spiritual battle with the unseen forces of darkness that are at the root of all false doctrines. They are the ones that need to be defeated. It is not necessarily the individuals of any cult group, including Jehovah's Witnesses. The problem lies with the spirits behind the cults. For example, Satan's main purpose has been to usurp God's authority and power. As he has pushed forward in this purpose, his tactics have never changed from the beginning of his rebellion, especially in regards to man. What are Satan's main tactics? His main tactic is to present himself as something non-threatening. The next step is to pervert God's words through deception and lies and make them appear as the truth. The third step is to make the perversion appealing to the flesh.

But, in addition to knowing what Satan's tactics are, we need to talk about how he uses them to achieve another goal.

Satan's goal from the Garden of Eden has been to kill the Messiah, the Christ-to kill Jesus. He was always watching and waiting for Jesus to appear so he could destroy Him. He thought he had done that very thing at Calvary; instead, it brought about his ultimate defeat. But, has this stopped Satan? No! He still needs to kill Jesus somehow in order to kill the message of hope, salvation, redemption, and God's promise to mankind of everlasting life with Almighty God in heaven. How does Satan accomplish this? He kills Jesus through the doctrines of the cults under the guise of organizations like the Watchtower Society who deny the deity of Jesus or through world religions who don't recognize Him at all. This is where Christians can see the forces of darkness at work: no matter what a cult believes, everything hinges on the teaching that Jesus was ultimately just a human being who was humanly exalted. In regards to Jehovah's Witnesses, Jesus had/has no deity whatsoever. The end result is that the full importance of who Jesus was, what Jesus taught, His suffering, His death, His blood, and His resurrection were all perverted. In essence, they have "...trampled the Son of God underfoot, counted the blood of the covenant by which he was sanctified a common thing, and insulted the Spirit . ." (Hebrews 10:29 NKJV). So why should we have compassion on Jehovah's Witnesses?

I know from firsthand experience that many honest and sincere people, Jehovah Witness believers, actually believe Satan's lies through that organization. They truly believe that they are serving Jehovah God with spirit and truth. The really sad part is that Satan and his minions have them totally in bondage by the belief that separation, isolation, and insulation from anything truly Christian is the way God intends for them to be. But, this situation is like a two-edged sword.

Most Christians find J.W.'s doctrines, beliefs, and preaching methods so offensive and repulsive that they lend to their isolation by not talking to them. Specifically, most of us have given up trying to speak the Gospel to them. This is not a reproach or condemnation on Christians. I believe that this lack of interchange has served in many ways to protect many Christians through the dark and troublesome times of the past few decades.

This lack of communication between Christians and J. W's also brings us to some important things we must face about ourselves. The fact is that the majority of Christians do not know what they believe or why they believe it. Thus, they are unable to give a proper defense of the Gospel. The lack of biblical knowledge leaves these people susceptible to a cult's message because they don't have anything to compare it with.

Secondly, few religious leaders have really wanted to educate Christians about the basic beliefs and doctrines of the sects and cults. Believe it or not, this often leaves people dangerously open to curiosity about these organizations. Thirdly, many Christians who know the Bible, as well as the major Christian doctrines, sincerely have the strong desire to share their faith but are unable to. Nearly all of the latter people end up with some degree of emotional stress because they think that they have somehow let God down. These issues are what this book is all about.

It's about loving, serving, and glorifying God out of a grateful heart. It's about helping spiritual brothers and sisters by instructing and informing them on how to take the believer's power and authority given through Jesus Christ by the Holy Spirit in order to make a solid defense to Jehovah's

Witnesses. It is about protecting them and their families from the wolves in sheep's clothing. It's about all of us being Christ-like in love, patience, and caring about the spiritual condition of others-of Jehovah's Witnesses. In short, it is about planting seeds. However, before we go any further, perhaps we should talk about something else-change.

Why Change?

To many people change is a scary word, isn't it? Most of us don't like change. We all know that adjustments and changes are not always easy or even desirable. We like to stay within our comfort zone, where we feel safe and secure. However, the changes I'm talking about should not be too painful if we're really serious about serving God. The facts are that many Christians will need to make a change in their attitudes and understanding.

One important area that I know many Christians need to make a change in is why they reject and object to Jehovah's Witnesses in the first place. This is not in a spirit of reproach, but at least 90% of all objections regarding Jehovah's Witnesses have been: they don't serve in the military, they don't celebrate birthdays or holidays, and they don't take blood transfusions. I'm not addressing whether these beliefs are right or wrong, rather, isn't something missing here? Where is God in these objections? Where are the Christian doctrines that should be the foundation of why the Witness' beliefs are wrong? Christianity is all about Jesus, so where is He mentioned in all this? I believe that sincere Christians will agree with me that we need to start digging into the spiritual heart of the matter. A good reason for doing this is because I know that people's/society's ostracism concerning the matters mentioned above barely makes a small dent in a

J.W. In fact, most of them expect these objections because they've heard them for so long. What they're not accustomed to is having other people know what their beliefs and methods are. Nevertheless, these objections are not the only thing that need adjustment.

Another important area that needs change is the Christian's general attitude about J.W.s. The dominant idea for many decades has been that if you're a Jehovah's Witness, somehow you are not worthy of any consideration for salvation. It's like you're a plague to be avoided at all costs. I feel that the biggest reason for this perspective is a lack of understanding. People just don't understand that Jehovah's Witnesses on the human level are *ordinary people* who are enveloped in spiritual darkness. I discovered in painful ways that a very fine line exists between condemning what a person believes and condemning the person. I'm an ordinary person now and an ordinary person when I was a Jehovah's Witness. Let me give you an example.

When I was a Jehovah's Witness, my grandmother told me that she was at church one day and she was telling her church friends about how nice, faithful, and loyal I was in helping her, picking her up and bringing her to church, taking her to the doctor and grocery shopping, visiting, and bringing her to our home on a regular basis for dinner. Do you know what their Christian response to her was? "But she's a Jehovah's Witness!" It didn't matter that I was one of God's creatures or that I was morally clean. They gave no other reason whatsoever for their condemnation, rejection, objections, or whatever else you want to label it, other than, "She is a Jehovah's Witness." Her feisty response to them was, "She may be a Jehovah's Witness, but I love her anyway!"

That was many years ago and I do not harbor any hard feelings toward anyone about their thoughts or words about me. But, I never forgot my grandmother's response, and it made me love her more. It also made me love God more since I know this is exactly how He saw me-I was in err, I was in spiritual darkness, but He still loved me and waited for the day that I would turn to Him with my whole heart, mind, and soul. After all, isn't that what Jesus died for?

But let's extend the subject of understanding a little further. I believe that many Christians may feel that seeing J.W.s as real people might mean compromising one's Christian beliefs. It absolutely doesn't mean this at all. If I didn't learn anything else from my experiences, I came to realize that there is a huge difference between hating/condemning doctrine and methods and loving the person who is in God's image beneath it all. That's exactly how Jesus sees people.

Jesus walked among all types of sinners such as harlots, adulterers, thieves, liars, users, manipulators, and false teachers. And He did more than that, too; He talked and preached to them, taught them, ate with them, and healed many of them spiritually and physically. I believe we are supposed to have a Christ-like walk and talk. But let's take a look at some early Christian examples of change.

One Christian we can look at is the apostle Peter. When the Holy Spirit directed him to go to Cornelius' house as recorded in Acts 10, we discover that Peter's objections were based on his Jewish beliefs that Cornelius was an unclean, gentile pagan. But he had an eye-opening experience when the Holy Spirit fell on the "unclean" person and his household just like it had on the Jews on the day of Pentecost. Peter had to understand that he had to look beyond what he thought about the outer person. He ultimately came to understand that it is Almighty God who knows the heart. He also found out that God's plans were not always what he expected them to be.

ruth baker

We can also look at another apostle, Paul. First, Paul was raised and schooled in the rigid teachings and rabbinical tradition of the Jewish faith. In addition to disliking gentiles and their beliefs (in regards to being outside the Israelite faith), he hated, persecuted, imprisoned, and was instrumental in executing many of the early Christians because he thought the new sect was going against God. He, too, had his eyes of understanding opened in several ways. The central idea I want to make, however, is that from Paul's conversion and for a number of years after that, he took the message only to Jews. But where did his ministry end up? Going into Gentile nations and preaching among and to violent "pagans," idolaters, and the sexually immoral-all of whom were steeped in false religion.

Ultimately, all the Jewish disciples, especially Peter and Paul, had to come to an understanding of what it was all about. They needed to understand what God's desires and plan were for all people. And what has always been God's desire and plan? He inspired the prophet Ezekiel to express His desire: "'Do I have any pleasure at all that the wicked should die?' says the LORD God, 'and not that he should turn from his ways and live?...For I have no pleasure in the death of one who dies,' says the LORD God. 'Therefore turn and live!'" (Ezekiel 18: 23,32 NKJV). Jesus later asserted what God's plan was for all time: "For God so loved the world that He gave His only begotten Son, that *whoever* believes in Him should not perish but have everlasting life" (John 3:16 NKJV). Jesus also taught us that we are to be the light of the world so others would praise the Father (Matthew 5: 14–16 NKJV).

In order for Peter and Paul to come to this understanding, they had to make significant changes in their attitudes. Sometimes it meant completely abandoning the old ways

20

of thinking-making an attitude adjustment. Both of these apostles tell us in their writings what they ultimately came to understand and believe in their hearts.

Peter says: "The LORD is not slack concerning His promise, as some count slackness, but is longsuffering toward us, not willing that any should perish but that all should come to repentance" (2 Peter 3:9 NKJV). He also says: "'…And do not be afraid of their threats, nor be troubled. But sanctify the LORD God in your hearts, *and always be ready to give a defense to everyone who asks you a reason for the hope that is in you, with meekness and fear*'" (1 Peter 3: 14, 15 NKJV).

Then Paul tells us:

> For there is no distinction between Jew and Greek, for the same LORD over all is rich to *all* who call on Him. For "whoever calls on the name of the LORD will be saved." *How then shall they call on Him in whom they have not believed? And how shall they believe in Him of whom they have not heard? And how shall they hear without a preacher?*
> Romans 10:12–14 (NKJV)

He also says: "*Let your speech always be with grace, seasoned with salt, that you may know how you ought to answer each one*" (Colossians 4:6 NKJV). So we can see that Peter and Paul had a breakthrough in understanding that took each of them out of their own attitudes and placed them in line with God's desires and plans. This is what I'm talking about in regards to present day Christians.

Perhaps, just perhaps, the Christian attitude toward Jehovah's Witnesses should be one of viewing their visits as an opportunity instead of a nuisance. After all, most evangelicals put great stock in world missions and living the Word in their everyday lives. Perhaps it is time to view J.W.s as the mission field standing at your door. What could be easier? You don't have to go anywhere in order to do your mission. They come to you! You don't have to have any funding. You have everything right in your home. You don't have to make a specific time commitment for three, six, or more months at a time. Rather, you can manage and control whether you spend ten minutes or two hours.

In addition to all of the above reasons concerning why we should change, it is very important to remember two things: *Jehovah's Witnesses have a feeling of superiority and great satisfaction when people cannot give an accounting for their faith.* They not only believe that they have more accurate knowledge, but that they also have God's guidance via angels in their ministry. In fact, they mock our God, *the one true God!* In their mind-controlled worldview, if Christians had the spiritual truth, we would be able to defeat them when they come to our doors. Just more proof to them, as far as they are concerned, that we are under Satan's control and not God's. Excuse me for my bluntness, but this has got to change!

The other thing to keep in mind is *rejection and persecution makes Jehovah's Witnesses stronger.* Do not underestimate what this statement means. They have a whole group of Bible verses that have been misapplied, but fully support the reasons, in their minds, why they are the brunt of mistreatment, rejection, and persecution from "outsiders," "the world." They will argue, after all, it is plainly written in the Bible that true believers will be hated and persecuted because of bearing God's name and also because they are no part of the world. Although it is not pleasant for anyone to undergo this type of treatment at any time, believe me when I say that it does serve to solidify their belief that they have the truth when people do not answer the door when it is clear that someone is home. When people rudely or quietly shut the door in their faces. When they are beaten, imprisoned, and killed (this has indeed happened in numerous countries in the last seventy years). However, we can utilize this knowledge of *their* attitudes and turn them into spiritual weapons by being non-aggressive and, do I dare say, kind to them when they call on us.

There is little doubt that most Christian people will need to go through some altering processes before they can reach that place of peace. I feel that the first beneficial step we should take on our road to personal change, *with Christian discernment and caution,* is understanding why people find Jehovah's Witness' messages appealing in the first place.

What appeal do Jehovah's Witnesses have?

It may surprise many readers that the majority of Jehovah's Witnesses, especially in the United States, came from mainline Christian backgrounds. These people may or may not have attended their churches; nevertheless, they professed to be Christians. The question has always been, "How did they get themselves into this mess in the first place?" The answer is not exactly simple. The appeal began with each individual and what he or she needed or desired at a particular time that they were called on by a Witness. Many of those needs arose more than forty years ago as a result of widespread social instability and change.

J.W.'s greatest appeal began in the 1960s as a result of social chaos resulting in a huge influx of new converts. For example, in 1966 there were only 500,000–600,000 dedicated members worldwide. Within approximately ten years, the membership had skyrocketed into the millions. It might be constructive to understanding their appeal if we begin with that decade.

People joined the Watchtower Society in record numbers because numerous social and religious issues acted as a catalyst for a chaotic society. Although few of the issues actually originated in the 60s, they came to a head during that decade. All of the following reasons for growth are not derived from my own analysis or opinion, but were commonly recognized by most Witnesses during that time period. One of the first issues that erupted into turmoil resulted from the changes in the Roman Catholic Church, which arose from decisions made by the Second Ecumenical Council held in 1962. That resulted in a large exodus from the Catholic faith. A great number of these disillusioned Catholics found consolation in the Watchtower's messages.

Another reason for the growth in the Jehovah's Witness ranks was the racial issue. A lot of the social turmoil that erupted in the 50s concerning race spilled over into the next decade. This unrest prompted presidents Kennedy and Johnson to inaugurate some racial policies and laws that presented some hopeful solutions to this problem. Equality still did not happen. These issues and programs occurred almost simultaneously with the Ecumenical Council. The Witnesses were consequently successful in gaining a portion of the non-militant Afro-Americans because of the equal opportunities that existed within the Watchtower organization. This equality was manifested in embracing them as social equals, which was a good thing. No one cared how much money they had, where they lived, where they came from, or what color they were. The Society also allowed Afro-American males to hold positions as ministerial servants or elders once they became mature in their knowledge and understanding. This was a reversal on a social, cultural, and religious level since Afro-Americans had been traditionally segregated in all of these areas.

Running concurrent with these two issues was the unpopularity of and protests over the Vietnam War. The Witnesses' appeal was that they didn't agree with any military conflict and didn't support or serve in any military capacity on the basis of conscientious objections. A number of other issues followed closely on the heels of the Vietnam War issue. These were the sexual revolution and the drug culture, which simultaneously burst upon the scene. The whole social climate was made more complicated as the family unit began to deteriorate and more divorces began to take place. We also need to mention that at this time illegitimate birth rates and abortions started to climb to new heights. The coup de grace of the sixties decade was that more and more people stopped going to church.

When you put all of these conditions together, many people from all walks of life were thrown into complete confusion of what was happening to them, to their families, to the United States-to the world. I'm sorry to say that there weren't too many authorities at any level giving people explanations or answers. Well, you have guessed what happened. Jehovah's Witnesses just did what they believed in, door-to-door ministry. They brought biblical answers with them, albeit false doctrines, that many people found comforting. These people whom the Jehovah's Witnesses evangelized became Jehovah's Witnesses who in turn started the ministry themselves. With these extra "ministers" from the mid-sixties, an extra boost occurred when the Watchtower Society predicted that Armageddon was going to occur around 1974.

All of these new converts during the mid-sixties to the mid-seventies resulted in natural growth. More members had families and raised their children to be Witnesses. The strong exhortation throughout the organization was that a Witness should marry a Witness. And so it continues up to the present time. You may say that was thirty to forty years ago. What does that have to do with their appeal today? Well, the answer is also in the form of a question: has the world gotten any better? It is clear that many of those social conditions still exist and many more issues have been added to them. We must also understand that we've been discussing overarching social factors that led to a growth in the Jehovah's Witness organization. We need to also look at some of the most common factors that appeal to people on an individual basis, then and now.

1. *The average person does not know what he or she believes.* This has been said before but it bears repeating. Oh, most people know about Jesus, God, and the Holy Spirit; however, it is usually on a name only basis. Most of these people also do not know or read the Bible. If they do, they don't understand it. Basically, they can't give you any reason for what they do know. This factor is something that Jehovah's Witnesses are well aware of, and they most often use peoples' ignorance of the Bible to the utmost degree. Thank God that most churches in the last ten to twenty years have started discipleship classes that educate parishioners in some doctrines. Still, the level of training is usually insufficient and does not trickle down to the church body as a whole; thus rendering Christians largely inept to deal with Witnesses on their doorstep.

2. *Jehovah's Witnesses use the same terminology as Christians do.* These terms include God/Father, Son/Jesus, spirit, baptism, salvation, redemption, resurrection, the Bible, etc. This leads most people who do not know God or the Bible into the false impression that they are just another Christian group doing good works. Another pitfall is that the Witnesses look just like you and me and appear non-threatening. The dangerous differences are in their

doctrines that lie behind the terminology and works. Unfortunately, these doctrines and beliefs are introduced so slowly that one easily slips into them without fully realizing it.

3. *A person has questions that have not been asked of a knowledgeable Christian.* If he or she has asked, they have not received a satisfactory answer-at least, not as far as that individual is concerned. These questions have usually centered on world troubles, death, social issues, equality, and a myriad of other questions as well. Here's where the Witnesses come in. They have an answer to everything.

4. *A person has a desire for law, order, and unity.* This is a common desire for many people who become interested in the Watchtower Society. They dislike the disunity and "political wrangling" that go on within the church. These types of people also see too many immoral behaviors going on within various congregations. Too often, when this type gets so disgusted with the condition of their local church, they stay home. Now they are "ripe for the picking." I can tell you this is where Witnesses reign supreme. Let me explain a few examples.

When the subject is law and order, there is no doubt that the Watchtower Society wields complete and final authority over *every congregation and person.* No one can question or voice dissension with the governing board's decisions or actions. A person either accepts their authority in all respects or gets out.

If the subject is unity, the governing body dictates what everyone is to believe worldwide. They have exclusive rights to all biblical interpretation. But it goes much further than interpretation. They also dictate what, where, when, and how each congregation and every person is to think, behave, and believe. One of these areas includes their weekly meetings. Nearly all meetings are held at the same time on the same day of the week in every congregation all over the world. All congregations have the same Watchtower study article each Sunday. All Tuesday night small groups study the same book and try to maintain the same schedule for how much material is to be covered at each meeting. This is designed so everyone begins and finishes the book at the same time. All study books and Watchtower magazines have pre-framed questions for each paragraph to facilitate this progress. This method was devised so that all given answers are in keeping with Watchtower doctrines. No individual thinking, action, or biblical interpretation is accepted or tolerated. The repetitious nature of the material just keeps solidifying the teachings in everyone's head-this includes everyone from infants to the aged. A good thing to remember about their unity is that it is *worldwide without choice!* The main point about this law, order, and unity is that it is appealing to people with the desire to be followers. An indisputable fact has been that most people are followers. The problem is that few people understand that *it is completely authoritarian* and as time progresses the members are afraid to voice objections.

5. *I don't want to be rude.* This may seem much too simplistic and rather stupid on the face of it, but this reason actually did and still does happen today. I know this is true because this was my initial reason for beginning a Bible study with them. The older woman who called at my house was nice, friendly, and I truly thought she was just another Christian doing good works. As she called on me over a period of time, I talked to her and took the magazines. I didn't know the difference since I didn't know the Bible, let alone anything about doctrines. One day she asked me if I would

like to know more and have a book study. I didn't want to hurt her feelings so I said okay. Don't laugh. It's true. It was just as simple as that. The very same thing happens today. For example, in the spring of this year I was teaching a woman's Bible class at a local mission when I felt led to warn the ladies of the dangerous doctrines and methods of the cults. When I related my experience of why I started studying with a Witness, one woman was so amazed she immediately exclaimed that this was exactly the same reason she had started a Bible study with a Witness before she came to the mission. So, as foolish as it may seem, decades have passed but the same human response is still at work.

6. *Armageddon is coming!* A lot of people enter the Society whenever the governing board "gets a revelation" or they think they have finally made the correct calculation that Armageddon is to occur in a specific year. *The significance of this message is that anyone killed by God at Armageddon has no hope at all. You are annihilated forever with no hope of resurrection of any kind. You must get into Jehovah's Organization now before it's too late!* The main motivation for membership in the Society for these people, therefore, is usually based on fear for their own lives. Not surprisingly then, these people are generally the first to leave when Armageddon does not happen within a few years after the prediction fails. Unfortunately, many of them carry false doctrinal baggage and fear with them for the rest of their lives.

7. *The Crisis Experience.* This is listed last but it is by no means at the bottom of the list. Many people are completely devastated and without hope when faced with the death of a spouse or other loved one, a divorce, a cheating mate, dealing with rebellious children on drugs, or what-

ever. The greatest appeal to a person in this group is the hope Jehovah's Witnesses hold out. This hope falls primarily into two categories.

The first one is what I call the "second chance doctrine." This is especially appealing to someone whose loved one has died that was not "saved." Jehovah's Witnesses believe that if a person has died before Armageddon, he or she will definitely be resurrected onto the new earth for a training/testing period of 100 years. This 100-year period lies within the 1,000-year period of Christ's reign (this belief is explained more fully under the section entitled "Most Challenging Defenses"). The appeal lies in the enormous hope given to the grieving person of seeing and living with the loved one again, *right here on earth*. The dead have a second chance! But there is one condition. You, the non-Witness, must become and remain a faithful Jehovah's Witness or else die before Armageddon. The ultimate hope by extension is that you will not die at all since Armageddon is due to happen at any time. The basic belief is, concisely, if you don't die at Armageddon you will emerge into the new world order in your same fleshly body. It must be emphasized here that Satan's tactics can be seen at work in this doctrine-taking the fear of death and giving hope to the flesh, both to the living and dead.

The other hope for people is that God will soon completely do away with all grief, misery, sorrow, hurt, pain, social disorder, chaos, and evil. Again, Armageddon is just around the corner. You have to get in the organization now to avoid destruction.

As you can tell, most of these are age-old problems and issues that people throughout the millennia have experienced and have had to find ways to cope with them. The overall purpose has been to reveal that most people who become Jehovah's Witnesses begin life as ordinary, plain folk like everybody else. They just don't know what follows the J.W.'s initial contacts. In other words, there is a whole lot that transpires before a person is *transformed* into a baptized Jehovah's Witness.

The making of a
Jehovah's Witness

As stated above, the initial appeal of the Jehovah's Witness' doctrine can be as varied as people's personalities. It may still be a mystery to most outsiders (non-Witnesses) just exactly how someone can be "hood winked" into that religion. Let me tell you that it is a long, subtle process, and the change usually begins with a knock on the door.

As everyone knows, most of the initial contacts made with J.W.s are while they are in their door-to-door ministry. But what really precedes this contact? In any given two-week period of time, which coincides with the new issues of the *Awake!* and *Watchtower* magazines, there is a ministerial theme recommended by the governing body in New York City. This theme includes ways of presenting the magazines and the best scriptural passages to use in order to substantiate the article. These keynotes are discussed each time the main group that meets at the Kingdom Hall leaves for their ministry. An important thing for people to know is this is not a random ministry. It is highly organized and consists of plats of each township, town, city, countryside, street, and road that lie within the jurisdiction of each Kingdom Hall. These plats are then divided into separate grids. One person can sign for a grid and he or she is responsible for "working" that territory. That is accomplished by stopping at every home within that area. This is not just for a particular state within the United States only. It is worldwide for every continent, nation, country, town, or village. This is how they get organized before they come to your door. Now you should know what happens once they get there. Before I begin, I feel the need to caution everyone not to be too judgmental concerning what is following, for it may seem that they are "trying to trap you." You must realize that these people have the deep conviction that they are doing God's will. They feel that they are obeying God's command to help you learn the "truth" in order to, first, help ensure everlasting life for themselves, then for you to gain everlasting life. They are so convinced of their 'truth' that if God were to open the heavens and tell them that what they are teaching was wrong, most of them would drop dead from shock. I know I would have. Anyway, knock, knock. Jehovah's Witness calling.

First, they tell you that they are Christians making calls on people in your neighborhood. They usually don't tell you right up front that they are J.W.s. The next step is to engage you in some type of conversation concerning the dire social and world conditions we are all experiencing. These *questions are designed to get you to agree with them* that we're living in a world amid terrible social and moral conditions. It is also *to get you involved in the conversation.* They soon present the *Awake!* and *Watchtower* magazines and point to an article that runs parallel to the conversation that you're having. Many homeowners take these magazines for a variety of reasons including curiosity, interest, or just to get them to go away. *This is a mistake!* J.W.s don't care why you take the magazines! They know that few people will immediately throw the magazines into the trash. The probability is that one of their story lines or topics will sooner or later capture your attention and often lead to further interest. Then what do you do? You open up the magazine and start reading it. Why does this happen? Two reasons. First, the Society presents the written material in a very simple, direct, interesting way that can be easily understood even by people who have a low level of education. This is particularly true of the *Awake!* magazine.

The *Awake!* magazine centers on everyday problems and social/world issues. *Awake!* is almost invariably the magazine that is presented at the door (with the *Watchtower* magazine tucked beneath it). This is also the publication that more non-Witnesses are most likely to read because they are reading about common problems that have been solved by real-life people. The kicker is that the story is about a person who now belongs to the Watchtower Society. Bottom line-that was the reason the person was able to overcome the difficulty.

The second reason why interest is generated in the magazines concerns the graphics the Society incorporates into their materials. They stress that all talents should be used for the furtherance of the Kingdom message. This has resulted in the recruitment of very talented full-time artists. These pictorials can be beautiful, thought-provoking, and even fear-inspiring. If the pictures capture your attention, then you will open the magazine and read the articles. These are the motivations and goals in coming to your house, but now you need to know what immediately happens when they leave.

You may be surprised to know that nearly every Witness carries a pen or pencil and paper of some kind. Now what are these for? If you take any of their publications, these are used to record personal information that was gathered during the visit. This may include either one, some, or all of the following: which issues of the magazines have been placed at that home, the person's gender, marital status if known, sometimes the approximate age, what the conversation consisted of, whether any children or children's things were visible, the name, address, and anything else they think is pertinent for that call. It is also recorded if no one is home and if they have left any material in the door. It is not a coincidence that the same person usually calls back in about three to four weeks if you have taken the magazines. There is a plan behind the same person making repeated calls to the same house. It is to develop a relationship between the homeowner and the Witness. Familiarity. Friendship. They are aware of what they are doing but think they are doing the "right thing."

I must add here, though, there is usually one exception regarding gender that applies to the above situation. If a woman calls at a house and a man comes to the door and shows interest, that woman will either come back at a later time with a man or hand over the call entirely to a man. The vice versa is also true if a man makes contact with a woman. It is no secret that a woman relates to a woman's feelings, emotions, and problems, and men relate to men. This procedure is also designed to keep anyone from immoral temptations that could arise over time. There is yet another facet to their call that you should know about before we proceed to the second step. You may think that the following material concerning a J.W.'s ministerial time is all pretty boring. You may ask, "Why is it necessary to know these things at all?" *The purpose is to let everyone know that this is a work-based organization.* It operates, in effect, both as a trickle-down and a trickle-up theory. Knowledge, guidance, beliefs, rules, and regulations trickle down from the governing board in New York and ultimately reaches each congregation and each J.W. Then, each J.W. at the grass-roots level sends all of his time and production totals (it trickles up) to the governing board. This trickle up then makes it possible for the organization to boast about how diligent, blessed, and productive they are. The following is how it all works.

Every minute that any Jehovah's Witness spends in his ministry, including any calls at your home, is accrued time in witnessing. This time is not only spent in their door-to-door ministry, but may also include witnessing at a family gathering, during a visit with a friend, at a social gathering, with co-workers, with a neighbor in the yard, writing letters, during a phone call, or having Bible studies with new "converts" or with their own children. A desired minimum of ten hours a month in witnessing is stressed for each Witness. I might add that it's not always because one wants to or even likes in the least going out in "service." However, they will take every opportunity they can to accumulate hours. No one within the Society forces a person into the witnessing, but it's because you basically have to or else you feel that you're falling short of Jesus' command to preach and teach the gospel. You will also be "counseled" to get on the ball, so to speak. On the other hand, if a Witness signs up to be a full-time "pioneer," he is are obligated to fulfill 100 hours per month in the ministry.

In short, a running total is kept of every minute that each Witness speaks about Jehovah or the organization's beliefs, conducts a Bible study, and the total number of all magazines, books, or tracts they have left with people. Each Witness then turns their information into the congregation on a monthly basis. The "ministerial servant," who is responsible for these records at the congregation, then logs each member's hours on his personal record card. This card is reviewed by the congregation's elders and may be reviewed by the traveling district and circuit overseers as well. Next, each congregation sends the recorded corporate time for their Kingdom Hall to the Society in New York City. The Watchtower Society is then able to accurately publish how many ministry hours are being engaged in worldwide, how many magazines, books, or other materials have been placed, and how many book studies are being conducted.

These are not the only records sent to the Society. Detailed records are kept of how many people attend each meeting, how many full-time and part-time ministers they have, the number of new baptisms for each congregation, the death of a dedicated member, or anything else that may alter the Society's total literature, membership, or ministry numbers. They also record when a J.W. moves from one locality to another. They will notify the Kingdom Hall elders in the new location that you are in that territory. In short, they know where you are at all times.

I believe that it is appropriate at this juncture to insert one of my personal motivations for writing this book: If the Witnesses (or Mormons) are going to be out in their ministry, I prefer that they spend more time at my house instead of calling on someone else who is not prepared. In other words, I'm going to turn every opportunity and every minute of their time into a defense of the Gospel-for Jesus. And who knows, God might send someone to my door who will really benefit from an encounter with me. Or maybe with you when you are prepared.

What we have learned thus far about the J.W.'s methods can be considered their ground work-the preparation of the field. We will now turn to the second step in making a Jehovah's Witness. The second step in a person's transformation begins after a number of visits have been made, which have produced sufficient interest with the homeowner. The Witness consequently offers to come to the person's home for a weekly book study. This second stage begins when the offer is accepted. Now the initial seeds of indoctrination and transformation can be sown.

There are several phases that make up the second step. It begins with the personal home book study, which is conducted at least once a week for one hour. This book study is usually conducted by the person who has been calling on you for the past weeks or months. The book that a person starts to study from, like the ministry plats, is very carefully chosen. The governing body in New York makes a strong recommendation or decision at periodic intervals as to which book(s) should be used for beginning instructions. The teacher may then proceed at a pace that is comfortable for the potential convert. The recommended time for a complete study, which might involve studying several books, is six months. This period of time is sufficient to cover many or all of the basic doctrines and to gauge the person's reactions and progress.

If the person has made acceptable progress during this six-month period, the next phase is to invite him or her to the Tuesday night small group book study. These book studies are small groups from the same congregation and usually held in a member's home. The same book is studied worldwide. It is desirable to have a newly interested person go to one of these studies since it advances their knowledge, they meet other members, and it prefigures the Kingdom Hall meetings on a smaller scale. Same people, same behavior, same teachings. It is soon time for the next phase. The third phase is to invite them to the Kingdom Hall. This is an important step. It initiates them into what happens there, and it enables them to see the complete obedience and unity of everyone. A new con-

ruth baker

vert is generally not invited in the very early phases because the idea is to have them partially prepared before they get to the Kingdom Hall. This preparation helps to avoid any confusion on the newly interested person's part and to avoid any disturbance within the congregation.

This third phase also includes the admonition and invitation to accompany your teacher or one of the larger group in the door-to-door ministry. You are not expected to do any talking, just go along. Do I need to tell you why? It breaks them in as one of the group with no up-front pressure. I thought when I was asked to go that I would always have the choice on whether I actually went or not.

However, all during these phases there is no force and no coercion. That is why Jehovah's Witnesses will deny that they have brainwashed anyone or that they have been brainwashed themselves. They have not been, in fact, brainwashed, rather, the process is what I call mind control. Let me explain. Brainwashing techniques, as I understand it, involve isolation with intense, aggressive, and often forceful methods of indoctrinating someone into doing something they don't necessarily want to do or would do willfully. This is not the case with Jehovah's Witnesses. They let everyone make their own choices in the beginning. Each person has freely taken the magazines. Each one has decided to talk to the Witnesses. Each one has agreed to the book study. Each one accepted the teachings. Each one decided to go to the Kingdom Hall and out in the ministry. Each person decides where they go and what they do and say. But, you must continually exhibit change to their way of thinking, believing, and doing. If you don't measure up to their standards, they put you to the wayside. Yes, Jehovah's Witnesses' teachings and methods are very subtle and innocent. I still remember what my teacher told me decades ago-it is a biblical principle you know: be

42

cunning as serpents but innocent as doves. Nevertheless, they don't make any of the decisions for anyone. Basically, everyone drives the car to the edge of the cliff without knowing the end-of-the-road destination. Before you know it, you've lost complete control of your life. The Witnesses just guide and direct you regarding which turns to make along the way, most often by using guilt and fear.

This whole process works toward the fourth and final goal of baptism. Jehovah's Witnesses call it dedication because it is one's dedicating his life to God. It is full immersion baptism in the name of the Father, Son, and holy spirit (notice their use of small letters of the latter) as recorded in Matthew 28: 19–20 in their New World Translation of the Bible. It can't stand in any more stark contrast to Christian baptism, which is primarily the believer's immersion into Jesus' death and resurrection in the manner of His resurrection to show that salvation has already taken place.

Baptism is the most important step in the whole process for the Witnesses. It means that once baptized, you are *forever* a Jehovah's Witness. You are also a lifelong member of the Watchtower Society, which they consider to be God's faithful and discreet slave who dispenses God's food at the proper time. Baptism also helps to guarantee personal safety in the coming Armageddon and entry into the New Earth Order. In other words, baptism is a necessity to obtain salvation. Once baptized, the newly dedicated Witness has the responsibility of conforming to all the requirements put upon all Jehovah's Witnesses. He is expected to perfect ministry techniques in the training program, which normally takes place each Thursday evening. (This process is discussed more fully in the chapter "Witnessing Methods that Just Don't Work and Why.")

The impression I want to make in this section is that

this is an ongoing cycle. The people of yesterday became Witnesses because someone didn't warn them of the dangers of the Jehovah's Witnesses' teachings and methods. Someone failed in his responsibility to teach the real truth of God's Word. Now those people are out making new Witness disciples. Who is going to be the next one? Could it be your mother, father, sister, brother, husband, wife, daughter, son, niece, friend, or neighbor? You say that it couldn't happen to them, that it can't happen to you. All are Christians. Don't be so sure about that. It happened to me and my neighbor. I have seen churchgoers and members from nearly every Christian denomination sitting in the seats of a Kingdom Hall. And, yes, there have even been some former church leaders sitting there, too! You see, no one is immune from doubts, fears, or confusion. I admittedly do not know all the circumstances in all these cases, but I'll bet that most of them were enticed by one of the subtle methods mentioned above. It often takes just one instance of a Witness having an answer to a certain issue that you cannot give a response to. Why? Their "knowledge," their "wisdom and understanding," or their "sincerity" either awes you or makes you doubt the validity of your own beliefs. I feel that it is imperative that first, people learn Christian doctrine *and* second, know the beliefs and methodologies of the cults-Jehovah's Witnesses in this case. It is for you and your family's protection. This is not a game. Our attitude shouldn't be "it doesn't matter." It does matter. It isn't just who can prove the other one wrong in a religious debate. Two vital aspects are at stake for everyone, us and them: life and death. We must understand that God utilizes Christians to help others find this life by shedding light on J.W.s, or any other person steeped in false doctrines, when they come to our doors. This is an especially important assignment for us because not everyone who has gone through this transformation process is happy. Nevertheless, until the confused and discontented are enlightened by the real Truth, they still cling to Jehovah's Witness' beliefs.

Why do they stay in the organization?

The basic reason that people don't leave the organization when they think that Jehovah's Witnesses are wrong concerning some doctrine or rule is *fear*. There are four crucial elements that compose this fear that permeates their total mental and physical being. Sadly, J.W.s do not recognize this fear for what it truly is.

Fear of no Hope

It is almost incomprehensible for most people to fully understand how strongly it has been ingrained into every J.W. that once you have been taught the "truth" of God's Word and are baptized (dedicated), you are at once and always a Jehovah's Witness. They do not view your leaving for any reason as a rejection merely of the organization-it is the rejection of Jehovah God. If you do not repent, you are forever condemned. In fact, any person who leaves the organization is worse than anyone else on earth. The bottom line for an individual is that once you have become totally indoctrinated, you are convinced that if you leave the Watchtower Society, you will be completely alienated from God with no chance of eternal life. The fear that Armageddon is due to happen any second guarantees that you will die forever without being under the canopy of the Watchtower's protection. I know how sad, how awful, it is to be in that bondage.

Fear for Family

Every baptized and dedicated J.W. believes that every parent on earth is personally responsible for the salvation of his children from birth to age of accountability. If you reject Jehovah, He rejects and destroys both you and your minor children at Armageddon. The only alternate chance your small children have is if they die before Jehovah executes His judgment upon the nations at Armageddon. They would have to die because J.W.s teach that all who die, except the very evil, before Armageddon will be resurrected, at least for a time. Believe me. This is a terrible burden for a parent to carry. I know the impact the teaching has because it was this exact teaching that got me into the organization. And, it kept me there for a long, long time. I remember telling my teacher after I had studied for a good long while, but before baptism, that I didn't know if I wanted to continue studying. My reason was that I didn't know if I believed all their teachings. Then my teacher whom I loved and respected (she became closer to me than my natural mother) laid the above teaching on me with their supporting scriptures. I was a goner from then on. The only consolation I have is knowing that I'm not the only one who has been taken unawares because of love for my children. Who wants to be ultimately responsible for the condemnation and annihilation of their children? In spite of the wrongfulness of this belief, they truly believe that children will also be annihilated along with the parents.

Fear of Shunning

It is also difficult for the majority of people to fully understand the immense emotional impact that rejection and shunning have on a person. Jehovah's Witnesses teach and admonish that members of the Watchtower Society are "God's family." Not only are family holiday dinners discouraged, but so are contacts with non-Witness friends or co-workers outside of the work place. They go so far as to admonish and warn members not to attend any weddings and funerals if they are conducted inside a church. This admonition also applies to ceremonies that are held in a private home, etc., if they are to be presided over by mainline Christian clergymen. I might add that this also applies to funerals of one's own parents. It is not long, therefore, before you become distanced from the majority of contacts of any kind outside of the J.W. organization. J.W.s are first and last, your only true friends and associates.

How does this all fit in with shunning? Well, if you willfully leave, dissociate yourself, or become disfellowshipped, not one of them remains friendly to you. At the time I came into the organization, no one would even speak one word to a person who fell into one of the above conditions. You are basically left with nothing: You have no God, no hope, no eternal life, no family, no friends-no support system. If you work for another Jehovah's Witness, as so many of them do, then it means that you no longer have a job. A person is left with nothing but despair, bitterness, and most of all fear of life and Satan.

Fear of Satanic Attacks

The fear Jehovah's Witnesses have of Satan if they get outside the Watchtower Society cannot be expressed strongly enough. The entire organization from top to bottom believes, preaches, and teaches that leaving the Society will open you up to satanic attacks since you no longer have God's protection.

As odd as this may sound, it is true-*but* not for the reasons they say. I know! I will tell you in advance that some of you will not believe what you are about to read; some will believe, and others may scoff. That's okay because I know, God knows, that I am telling you the truth. I am willing to risk the ridicule because it is imperative that Satan's agenda is exposed. However, to get to my personal attacks, I have to begin with the end of my association with the Jehovah's Witnesses and their organization.

I left the Jehovah's Witnesses willingly in 1989. It all had to do with their continual endorsement that "they fear God because they love Him, they do not love Him because they fear Him." I know that this is not always the case since that is precisely the reason I left the organization. I literally got out of bed one day and something suddenly struck me. I can still remember the words that I uttered out loud: "Fear! Fear! Fear! That's all I feel is fear! Where is this God of love that the Witnesses talk about and I read about in the Bible? I don't know this God of love. Everything that I do out of fear and not out of love is all for nothing. I might as well forget the whole thing because I'm condemned already!" That feeling was so strongly pervasive that I never went back or had any association with the Witnesses from that minute forward. However, that wasn't the end of it all. I did not actually renounce it for another thirteen years. You see, I was still carrying around the psychological certainty of doom and destruction that I had absorbed all those prior years. Here's the really grievous part. In their opinion, nothing is ever the fault of the organization or leaders. There has got to be something wrong with the person. So I thought that there was something really wrong with me! I felt that I was condemned but still clung to the hope that maybe, just maybe, I might still have a chance somehow if I could ever get myself straightened out. There is no doubt that I was in a spiritual wilderness and experiencing all of the mental anguish that I described above for that entire time. I never went to another church except for a few funerals. Even then, I was frightened by the knowledge that I was sitting inside "Satan's Church." What if Armageddon occurred while I was there? But I didn't experience any demonic attacks during this entire time. The time came, however, when all of this changed.

I became a Spirit born-again Christian in mid-May 2001. It was less than two weeks later that the initial attacks began. There were three attacks in all: two physical and one spiritual. They were terrible and ferocious. Again, it is important that I relate these experiences at this point because *everyone needs to know how dangerous it is for someone to become involved with Jehovah's Witnesses or any cult-type religion.*

The first attack came on a Saturday morning, a few minutes after midnight. A couple of hours before that, my husband and I were visiting with relatives in the dining room when my throat started to feel scratchy. But it wasn't anything serious. When I got up at midnight, though, my throat was really sore. I went downstairs and crossed the dining room to go into the kitchen. When I got as far as the kitchen doorway, I started to violently cough. It felt as though my throat was literally ripping out. It was very painful. I walked back and forth not really knowing what to do. It hurt so badly when I coughed that I prayed to God for help, asking Him if He had anyone praying for me. I started for the kitchen again and when I reached the doorway again, another violent coughing spell hit me. The difference this time was that I coughed up large chunks of yellow infection out of my throat. Strangely enough, later that day I was able to eat, drink, and talk with very little discomfort at all. Although I was puzzled by the sudden onset and departure of this illness, I never once thought of it as a demonic attack.

The second attack came just about two weeks after the first one. It also had its onset a little after midnight. I was perfectly fine when I went to bed around eleven o'clock p.m. I had trouble sleeping, though, and got up and went down stairs. I crossed the dining room and went into the kitchen. By the time I got to the kitchen stove, I was so ill I could hardly stand up. Actually, I felt deathly ill from the inside out. I tried to find comfort everywhere possible: sitting on a hard chair at the table, on different types of chairs and sofas in the living room, and lying on the floor. Several times I went into the bathroom to vomit but either had dry heaves or just got up clear fluid. I was so sick that for the first and only time I prayed to God for something I never thought I would, "Please, God, help me! Please Father, Jesus, and Holy Spirit help me or send angels to help me! If for some reason you don't heal me, let me die!" I mean I was really sick.

A few minutes later, I crawled on my hands and knees into the bathroom. This time I vomited numerous one-inch and larger chunks of yellow infection. Now another amazing thing happened. I crawled back to the hallway and lay down thinking that I probably would not be able to stand the smell of my own breath because I was too sick to brush my teeth. But to my amazement, I lay on my stomach and my breath that bounced back from my pillow was sweet smelling! I can't tell you the smell because it was like something I'd never smelled before. But it was a sweet aroma!

At nine a.m. I was still ill and weak feeling, but nowhere near as sick as I had been in the early hours. Nevertheless, my husband and daughter thought that I should go to the doctor. So we went to the doctor and his diagnosis was that I had a severe type of virus. His prognosis was that I would not be able to eat solid food for at least a week and would be in bed for about two weeks. After we returned home, I did take it easy that day. But, lo and behold, the next day I not only ate and drank as usual but did my normal housework and laundry!

I still did not have the slightest inkling that it was really a demonic attack. That is until I was talking to our pastor, Mike, about these things and suddenly he said that it sounded like satanic attacks. Well, this gave me something to think over but I did not worry about it because I didn't know if it was true. Then came the big one.

A few months later, I was trying to accumulate some of the scriptures that Jehovah's Witnesses use to substantiate their beliefs. I turned to 2 Peter 2: 20–22, which are the main verses they use to show that people are really condemned if they turn away from the "truth." Something suddenly occurred that I had never expected, had never thought about, and had never seen in a movie, on TV, or read anything like it.

After I finished reading the verses, I looked up from the Bible, just to think for a minute. Suddenly, "something" came from out of the northeast corner of the dining room. I couldn't see it, but I could certainly feel it. *It was pure evil.* It also didn't feel anything like wind, but it came with lightening speed toward me. I was absolutely terrified! It felt like it was settling on and enveloping me. I was completely frozen to the chair in fear! Then I could actually feel something start to wind around my waist me like a snake or a rope! All I could do was lift my right arm and cry out for help, "Oh, God, help me!" The "thing" almost immediately started to loosen its grip on me. It went away, and I have not had another physical attack that I'm aware of since then, which was more than four years ago.

I have taken the risk of telling you these events because it is so important to understand what happens to some people who break from Jehovah's Witnesses. It takes courage to tell anyone because of the fears that people will think you are crazy. Nevertheless, it is so important that I have related these things to others as well, including a master's seminar on cults attended by church pastors, church leaders, and others.

In addition to these points, I want to stress another fact: *God often keeps things hidden from us for our own good.* God only revealed to me the full impact of these events less than six months ago. First, I was indeed under demonic attacks in 2001. Secondly, I realized that all three of these attacks began suddenly in the dining room. Why? That is where the evil spirit had its "dwelling place." Third, even though I am a rational, intelligent, well-educated person, I did not recall the Witness' teaching about probable attacks if one left the organization. Why? My answer was in Exodus 13:17: "Then it came to pass, when Pharaoh had let the people go, that God did not lead them by way of the land of the Philistines, although that was near; *for God said, "Lest perhaps the people change their minds when they see war, and return to Egypt"* (NKJV).

Now you may wonder what on earth does that verse have to do with anything I've told you. Well, God is wiser than all. He knew that if I remembered the Witnesses' teaching on satanic attacks that I would undoubtedly have returned to the organization because it would appear that they were right. Also, He consequently kept hidden from me the number and severity of the attacks so that I would not be in constant fear. He wanted me to rely on Him whenever these events occurred. He also knew that I wasn't that strong in the faith yet. He also knew if I suspected at that time that a demon was living in that house, I would have been out of that place in a split second!

The greatest knowledge that I received from these attacks, especially the third one, is that we have something in us that is more powerful than *anything*-Satan or Jehovah's Witnesses! I have continually testified that if it had not been for the Holy Spirit in me that day that I would have been a raving lunatic that very same day. But, Hallelujah, God had His protective hedge over me, and the evil spirit could not get in! Overall, I came to the full realization that we have a spiritual battle with dark, unseen forces that want nothing less than to harm, possess, or kill us through sickness and the actions of others. I know firsthand that Satan and his cohorts are the original terrorists and will use all means available to entangle us in a web of deceit to keep us in the shadows of enslavement.

Ultimately, we must understand that Satan uses organizations such as Jehovah's Witnesses to pervert God's real truth and lead people into spiritual darkness. This robs God's glory, destroys pure worship, and diminishes the chance for eternal life. Satan also knows when an ex-Jehovah's Witness discovers the real truth and experiences the Holy Spirit, that person is a danger to him. He or she will expose the falseness of the J.W.s doctrines. Satan also knows that God will have one of the most zealous believers there is. Consequently, once someone has been "snared," Satan does not want to release him from his influence. So, he uses spiritual attacks to terrorize people back into his fold.

I also want you to know that although I haven't had physical attacks, Satan and his cohorts don't give up so easily. A person, at least it is so with me, stays under demonic assaults of a different nature for a long time. I'll relate a couple of examples.

More than two years ago, my husband and I went with some other couples in his family to visit their aunt in a nursing home. When we got there, we all went to a lounge so we could have a place to sit. After a while, we heard bone-chilling shrieks coming from somewhere down the hall. However, they kept getting closer and closer to the lounge. I said there must be some person who is having a hard time today. My husband's aunt said that it was a woman, and she was carrying on like that all the time. In fact, she said that the woman would go into the residents' rooms and terrorize them. It wasn't long until the woman made her way to the lounge's double doorway. She never crossed over into the room but just sat there in her wheelchair. We all looked at her but just thought that she was just another poor soul afflicted with mental illness. Suddenly, she looked straight at me and pointed her finger at me and said in a loud voice, "I know who you are. We don't want you here!"

I want to tell you that I will never forget that experience. Her eyes were full of hatred. Every hair on my body felt like it was standing on end, like I'd stuck my finger in a light socket. Not only that, but I also found out what it really meant to have your skin crawl. It felt like my skin was actually rippling, moving on my bones. I'm not talking about goose bumps, either. I thought to myself, *Lord, is this woman possessed or what?! Please make her be quiet.* She did become quiet, and it wasn't long until an aide came and took her back down the hall. When my husband and I left the place, I told him how I had felt when the woman said that to me. I wondered if she really had an unclean spirit of some kind. I didn't know for sure since I hadn't had anything happen like that before. I never told another person about that experience at that time. About a month later, my doubts concerning the origin of the woman's words turned into concrete evidence.

My church had an evangelist from England come for a revival. I never told him anything about the nursing home experience at all. One day, he was preaching and said that he made a lot of calls at nursing homes and informed the congregation that not all people in there are suffering from mental deficiencies. He said all he had to do was walk down the hall and he would hear someone growling, "Grrr. Grrr." He'd look in the room and the person would be wringing their hands and saying, "We know who you are and we don't want you here!" Does that sound familiar? I knew in an instant that my experience was real. That was my first experience with this type of confrontation, but not the last.

I have taught a woman's Bible study at a local faith mission over the past few years. During this time, there have been numerous women living at the mission that were raised as a J.W. or were dedicated Witnesses, as well as other women who came from radical sects that were on the outer fringes of true Christianity. Almost invariably the spirit that accompanies these people causes a disturbance and tries to cause trouble for me. I've had some get angry, yell, stomp out, and make complaints that I was a false teacher and a blasphemer. Now if you consider blasphemy telling the women that Jesus is God, God's name is probably Yahweh and not Jehovah in its Hebrew form, and that the King James Version of the Bible is not the only one that a Christian can use, I confess that I'm guilty. The bottom line is they can't bear to hear the true Word of God.

The whole truth is that when one of these cult believers comes into my class, they make themselves known the first or second time they're in the class. I sometimes found these occurrences disturbing, but now I really see this as one of my jobs. The reason I feel this way is some of the women over the years have told me that those that belong to the non-traditional churches and cults espouse their beliefs to all the residents. The Bible study consequently gave me the opportunity to address these doctrines and teachings. That can't be all bad. I'm not saying the other teachers are not speaking the truth, but let me tell you an example of how this all works.

Just five days ago, I was conducting a study when one of the other teachers unexpectedly came in and sat through the study. When it was over, she said what a good study it was. However, she expressed surprise that a Jehovah's Witness woman at the mission talked and asked questions throughout the entire study. These questions were posed in such a way that they could cast doubt on Christian doctrines. In addition to this, the J.W. woman, the other teacher, and I sat talking for one full hour afterward. The other teacher expressed surprise when we left the mission that the woman had talked so much. According to her, the J.W. always sat meekly and quietly through her study sessions.

The bottom line is that I no longer get too surprised at these types of conduct. I rather expect them. In my perspective it shows that the Spirit is with me and the truth is getting spoken. I will continue on as long as I can, because Jesus in me will not be defeated because of fear.

All in all, I wish to convey that Jehovah's Witnesses have a thorough saturation of teachings based on fear that keep members in line and within the fold. The most destructive and entangling aspect of their teachings are those that promote fear of leaving because the only safety they have is to stay within the Society. Safety from permanent alienation and condemnation in God's sight. Safety because membership in The Watchtower Society promises you life, and more importantly, the safety and eternal life of your small children. Safety from demonic attacks. Safety from "pollution" from the world, worldly people, and worldly family members. So, you see, the stronghold of fear and safety permeates the entire physical, emotional, and spiritual being of a Jehovah's Witness. We need to pity these people and offer them every hope God holds out through His Word. It is the only way that they can find freedom. Before we get into what works in accomplishing this goal, we need to know what methods are usually ineffective.

Witnessing methods that just don't work and why

This chapter is probably the most important information a Christian can have in order to adequately understand the closed mind of a Jehovah's Witness. I know there are many Christians who not only want to give a proper defense of the Gospel, but also want to extend spiritual help, spiritual help that leads to salvation and eternal life. Too often, though, Christians get angry, frustrated, and disheartened because every avenue that is taken seems to meet a rebuttal or refusal of some kind. Nothing seems to work. Here are a few methods Christians have used that just don't work and why.

Religious Handouts /Literature

Have you ever tried to give Christian literature of some type to a Jehovah's Witness? Or have you told them you will take their material if they take yours? If you have, you know first-hand that they refuse it. But why?

Their first response to you may be they don't need it.

While J.W.s do believe that they have the only true belief, it goes much deeper than that. Once again, it is fear grounded in their false doctrine. Let me explain since I've been there and done that.

Jehovah's Witnesses have a well-developed doctrine based on Babylon the Great as recorded in Revelation 14: 8 and Revelation 17. They teach that Babylon the Great, the harlot who sits on a many-headed, scarlet colored beast, is Satan's worldwide organization of false religion. This empire of false religion has adulterated herself with governments and the world in general. It is full of false worship, idolatry, idolatrous symbols, and demons. But who or what constitutes Babylon the Great in their reality? You may have guessed it already: Every religious belief and denomination in the world with the exception of Jehovah's Witnesses, whether it is Christian or non-Christian. It then extends to include each person belonging to these so-called false religions.

Therefore, when one of them comes to your door and you say you have your own belief and church, they instantly and subconsciously identify you with Babylon the Great- with Satan's organization. In their strong conviction, that also means your literature is Satan's vehicle to promote false religious teachings.

So, this is the way it goes. They will preach to you because of Jesus' command to go into the world and make disciples. They also feel that placing the written word through their literature will open the door of setting you free from Satan's clutch. However, they will not take any of your material because they have been thoroughly programmed not to take any religious material. To do so would leave them open to possible delusion and demonic attack. It would be a rare occurrence for any one of them to even touch it because it would make them guilty by association and transfer. Let me recap the following main points for clarity, just in case I haven't explained it clearly enough along the way:

1. Jehovah's Witnesses believe that all belief and religious systems except theirs is Satan's religious empire, Babylon the Great.
2. All people who believe in any religion but theirs are in spiritual darkness and under Satan's control.
3. All religious materials, symbols, rites, etc., are satanic.
4. For any J.W. to take part in any way, e.g., taking religious publications, puts them in danger of possibly falling prey to Satan.
5. They are endangering their eternal life by taking material because it opens them up to abandoning God's true religion and organization, which leads to separation from Jehovah. If this happens, then it results in bringing God's wrath and eternal destruction upon them at Armageddon.

Consequently, the efforts of many well-intentioned people who write up pamphlets, books, etc., to give J.W.s at the door are usually in vain. I'm not accusing anyone of trying to scam Christians. It's just that most people do not understand why a Witness will not take the literature regardless of what it may be-whether it is free or you take their literature. The truth is plain and simple-Jehovah's Witnesses simply will not take them because they perceive them as a potential satanic foothold.

Personal Testimonies

Let me say first of all, that personal testimony of God's work in anyone's life is powerful. Essentially, experience is greater than any other type of argument that can be made. It brings glory to God by showing how His mercy, power, and grace have worked and are still working. I'm not advocating that personal testimonies are useless. I do not aspire to stand in the place of God. You must let personal prayer and the Holy Spirit be your guide. Testimonies, nevertheless, are greatly ineffective with Jehovah's Witnesses as a whole. Why?

Again, their mind is almost totally closed when you speak of supernatural experiences. This condition also stems from a deeply ingrained false doctrine regarding the Holy Spirit. Jehovah's Witnesses believe that the Holy Spirit is not a person or being of any kind. Rather, they claim the Spirit is God's power that God pours out upon whomever and whenever He desires. They explain God's power, or to use their phrase "God's active force," as a force such as lightning or electricity. It comes and it goes, but never stays in one place and is never in all places at the same time. Thus He created, anointed, destroyed, led, and gave inspiration by this force.

I could go into many details about their rejection of the Trinity doctrine, which is at the bottom of this doctrine. However, I must keep this section simple and to the point: What is really behind their rejection of your personal testimony?

Jehovah's Witnesses do not believe, as I stated above, that the Holy Spirit is a separate living entity that is all-knowing, all-powerful, or ever-present. Nor do they believe that any of the spiritual gifts such as tongues, healing, prophecies, etc., are given to people today.

They believe that God initially poured out His power,

or spirit, on the apostles and the remaining number of the 120 people in the upper-room on the day of Pentecost. These were then empowered with the gifts mentioned such as apostleship, prophecies, tongues, etc. God then dispensed nothing further. All consequent, supernatural acts were carried on by the people from the upper-room but predominately through the apostles' laying on of hands to transfer the power gifts and the gospel to other people. J.W.s also believe that all persons that the apostles laid hands on could also do miracles. But when the apostles and those they laid hands on died, the acts of God's power also died.

The end result is Jehovah's Witnesses consider that all spiritual gifts claimed to be manifested in anyone's life today are the works of Satan. This is how J.W.s believe Satan brings delusion on people as he performs "powerful signs and wonders," a sign of the end times. Here we have arrived at the same satanic position that has been the conclusion of so many of J.W.'s beliefs: Those people who make a claim to have had supernatural experiences are under Satan's control. You have been captured by Satan's power since he is the "angel of light" (2 Corinthians 11:14). You have become the devil's children because you are following his beliefs, signs, and wonders. The bottom line is, of course, they believe Satan's "light" has everyone but them bound in chains of darkness.

Consequently, Jehovah's Witnesses reject and tune out most of what is said concerning personal supernatural experiences.

Scriptures

How many times have Jehovah's Witnesses come to your door and you have tried to read or quote scripture to them but it seems to go nowhere? In fact, how many times have the conversations basically escalated into an argument about who is right? Most often you are left frustrated, stymied for answers to them, angry, and determined to get out "the bomb" for their next visit. Come on now, you know it's true. You are often left wondering where you went wrong-why didn't this work? There are basically two reasons for their closed mind to your scriptures: The J.W.'s Bible-The New World Translation of the Holy Scriptures (this translation will most often be referred to hereafter as NWT) and their comprehensive training programs.

The New World Translation of the Holy Scriptures

The New World Translation of the Holy Scriptures was directed by Mr. Knorr, a president of the Watchtower Society. I don't know the exact date, but I believe that the new translation was completed sometime in the 1940s. What I do know for sure is that every Witness from that day forward has considered it the only true translation of the Bible that exists. This is the only Bible you will find in a Witness' home. Consequently, every person who starts a new Bible study with them is also encouraged to get a New World Translation. This exhortation is reinforced by the claim that there is no difference between the NWT and other Bibles, with the exception that they use the name Jehovah where it is supposed to be. That piece of goods was presented to me and I bought it because I didn't know what the Bible said anyway. I just accepted their word for it. I can tell you today after much prayer, reliance on the Holy Spirit, God seeking, and intensive study that their claim is emphatically and totally false. I believe that the most effective way to see why using scripture is largely ineffective when talking to Witnesses is to see what a few of their beliefs are, how the New World Translation upholds these beliefs, and how the New World Translation compares with the New King James Version.

1. They use the name Jehovah hundreds of times in the New Testament. Technically, according to every well-known Bible scholar, Jehovah is a man-made word and doesn't appear in the Hebrew or Greek of either the Old or New Testaments. However, while some translations have rendered the Hebrew YHWH as Jehovah a couple of times in the Old Testament, YHWH never appears in the Greek manuscripts of the New Testament. J.W.s claim that using "Jehovah God" in New Testament passages where only "God" occurs in the original Greek text is merely to give due respect to God's name. It is also to show Him as the one and only supreme God. Here lies one of their true motives in using Jehovah where it does not exist: It is to underscore their doctrine that there is no Trinity doctrine as Christians believe.

    Comparison Examples: The New King James Versions quotes Matthew 1:22 as: "So all this was done that it might be fulfilled which was spoken by the LORD through the prophet, saying." In contrast, the New World Translation states Matthew 1:22 as: "All this actually came about for that to be fulfilled which was spoken by Jehovah through his prophet, saying." The New King James Version also quotes Matthew 4:7, "'...You shall not tempt the LORD your God.'" In contrast, the New World Translation states Matthew 4:7 as: "'...You must not put Jehovah your God to the test.'"

2. They use the words "torture stake" instead of "cross." Their foremost objection for not using the word "cross" is that it was a pagan religious symbol used centuries before Christ. They also have the explanation that the Greek word that other translators render as "cross" can

also be translated "stake." I don't know that this translation is completely wrong. However, they not only translate it this way, but also teach it both in words and pictorial representations that Christ was hung on one straight, upright pole with His hands nailed above His head and His feet nailed below. They also claim that being crucified involved a slow, agonizing death, constituting torture. If I saw and heard this once, I saw and heard it hundreds of times. Regardless of these claims, there are two elements that they don't tell a newly-interested person about.

One element is the historical record concerning Roman crucifixion. In contrast to the J.W.'s teaching of a torture-stake, the Romans had several different types of wooden structures they *commonly* used in this form of execution. None of them conformed to the single upright stake. Rather, they most often used two pieces of wood that were crossed in some fashion.

The other thing is I couldn't find any translation, any reference, any commentary, or any words that could possibly be translated as "torture" in relationship to any other word that could be possibly translated as "stake." I may not be a confirmed Greek scholar but I do know how to read Bible concordances and dictionaries, as well as other literature!

In addition to substituting the words torture stake, they also never use the word "crucifixion" or "crucify." They translate the Greek word as "impaling." I also cannot say that this translation is completely wrong. However, they have to distance themselves as far away from Christians' translations as possible in order to substantiate their doctrines. We do have to admit that Christianity has always depicted Jesus as crucified on the cross.

Nevertheless, J.W.'s stance on "torture stake" and the vilification of the cross underscores their doctrine that Christians are involved in false religious worship, using pagan symbols, using the cross as an idol (they consequently label us as idolaters), and Christians have a wrong translation of the Bible. Need I say more? The comparison example of the NKJV and the NWT translations given below shows how the mental image of the crucifixion changes entirely.

Comparison Examples: The New King James Version quotes Matthew 27:31–32 as: "And when they had mocked Him, they took the robe off Him, put His own clothes on Him, and led Him away to be crucified. Now as they came out, they found a man of Cyrene, Simon by name. Him they compelled to bear His cross." In contrast, the New World Translation states Matthew 27:31–32 as: "Finally, when they had made fun of him, they took the cloak off and put his outer garments upon him and led him off for impaling. As they were going out they found a native of Cyrene named Simon. This man they impressed into service to lift up his torture stake."

3. J.W.s use the translation "a god" instead of "God" in such passages as John 1:1 and John 5:18 to disprove that Jesus was part of the Triune God or even claimed to be. I found so many biblical scholars who emphatically stated that the Watchtower's translations of these such phrases are incorrect that I don't need to cite any sources because it would be considered common knowledge to those who read about it. Just one of the reasons for the inaccuracy is the J.W.'s use of the indefinite article "a" where one is not indicated. The majority of Greek scholars also agree that the context of the original Greek shows that the word is to be translated as the supreme deity—God.

Comparison Examples: The New King James Version quotes John 1:1 as: "In the beginning was the Word, and Word was with God, and the Word was God." In contrast, the New World Translation states John 1:1 as: "In [the] beginning the Word was, and Word was with God, and the Word was a god."

4. J.W.s use "obeisance" where other Bibles read "worship" in relation to Jesus such as Matthew 28: 9 and John 9: 38, as well as many other scriptures. There is a huge difference between these two terms. Obeisance means to bow before someone to show respect or deference, for example, to an ordinary person like one's father or to a political dignitary. Worship means to pay reverence or homage to, especially to God. Since J.W.s claim that Jesus was the Son of God, but not God, He would never allow people to worship Him. Thus, they teach all of their followers that people just bowed or knelt before Jesus as an act of respect, to pay Him honor, or as recognition that he, as the Son of God, was in a higher position than they were.

Again, my research proved them wrong. The original Greek word has not been translated as obeisance at all in the New Testament but rather The New Strong's Exhaustive Concordance of the Bible reveals that the word translated as "worship" is *proskuneo*. Interestingly, according to this source, this Greek word's origin is probably derived from the words that mean "to run forward" and "to kiss, like a dog licking his master's hand; to fawn or crouch to, i.e., (literally or figuratively) prostrate oneself in homage (do reverence to, adore)-worship." When you look at the context of the passages I used above, that is exactly what Mary Magdalene and the healed blind man were doing, worshiping Jesus. Anyhow, Jehovah's

Witnesses use *obeisance* to uphold their doctrine that Jesus is not God and never was worshiped by anyone.

Comparison Examples: The New King James Version quotes Matthew 28:9 as: "And as they went to tell His disciples, behold, Jesus met them, saying, "Rejoice!" So they came and held Him by the feet and worshiped Him." In contrast, the New World Translation states Matthew 28:9 as: "And, look! Jesus met them and said: "Good day!" They approached and caught him by his feet and did obeisance to him." Another example is that the New King James Version quotes John 9:38 as: "Then he said, "LORD, I believe!" And he worshiped Him." In contrast, the New World Translation states John 9:38 as: "Then he said: "I do put faith [in him], LORD." And he did obeisance to him."

5. The NWT uses other ways to downplay Jesus' deity. In scriptures that speak of Jesus' role in creation, they use the words "through" and "by means of" instead of "by" such as in Colossians 1:16. Many people may think that this isn't any big deal, but it is. The context in which J.W.s use the terms undermines Jesus' supreme role as God and Creator.

Another blatant change they have made in their New World Translation is by inserting the word "[other]" in verses that speak of Jesus as Creator. They are exposing themselves by putting it in brackets, which clearly reveals their acknowledgment that they have inserted the word where it doesn't exist in the original text. You might have the same question that I had. If the Word (Jesus) created everything in heaven and earth, what were all the 'other' things? The Watchtower Society's answer is everything besides himself. Their doctrine states that He was the first created being and God merely bestowed the honor upon Jesus/Michael of helping create everything else.

J.W.s base their doctrine on the Bible writers' use of the word "firstborn" in relation to Jesus. Before we go any further, however, I believe that we must discover what the Christians' correct understanding of the word "firstborn" really is so that there is no confusion.

The word "firstborn" is really used in a two-fold way in the biblical sense. The first meaning, which is at the center of this discussion, must be understood from a historical perspective of Israelite/Jewish customs and laws. The law was that the firstborn son in a family was to be honored above the sons born later. Simply put, the firstborn son was to receive a greater inheritance regarding money and land. Head leadership of the family was also bestowed upon him by the father at the proper time. This is how it applies to Jesus. Jesus was not only God's firstborn son but His "only begotten Son," when Jesus (the second person of the trinity known as the Word of God) was incarnated into the womb of Mary by the Holy Spirit. He was then born in the flesh. Consequently, Father God bestowed upon Jesus, the firstborn of God, the preeminence of supreme honor, power, and the total inheritance above all creation. In other words, all of creation in heaven and earth was and always will be Jesus' inheritance; and as the firstborn son, the Father made Him the supreme head of God's children or "family"— all born-again Christians. The other meaning was that Jesus held preeminence over all creation since He was the firstborn from the dead when He was bodily resurrected and received everlasting life.

We can see how the New World Translation upholds

their doctrine by comparing translations of a relevant scripture.

Comparison Example: The New King James Version quotes Colossians 1:15, 16 as: "He is the image of the invisible God, the firstborn over all creation. For by Him all things were created that are in heaven and that are on earth, visible and invisible, whether thrones or dominions or principalities or powers. All things were created through Him and for Him." In contrast, The New World Translation states Colossians 1:15, 16 as: "He is the image of the invisible God, the firstborn of all creation; because by means of him all [other] things were created in the heavens and upon the earth...All [other] things have been created through him and for him."

6. The NWT has been translated to uphold J.W.'s doctrine that there is not an eternal place of punishment in a fiery hell. Thus, they use the phrases such as "into everlasting cutting off" in passages such as Matthew 25:46. This expresses their belief that Jehovah's punishment for the unrighteous is just complete annihilation. The fire and torment in their view are used to symbolize God's judgment of no life, which by extension means eternal separation from God by having no existence.

   Comparison example: The New King James Version quotes Matthew 25:46 as: "And these will go away into everlasting punishment, but the righteous into eternal life." In contrast, the New World Translation states Matthew 25:46 as: "And these will depart into everlasting cutting-off, but the righteous ones into everlasting life."

7. J.W.s use "holy spirit" with small letters instead of "Holy Spirit." Alongside of what I've stated before, J.W.s claim it is merely Jehovah's impersonal power force. By using

the small letters, they are showing that there is no deity whatsoever attached to the Holy Spirit. One official argument they use is that the Greek word for Spirit is neuter and does not have to be used in a masculine gender but can be referred to as an "it." They also try to refute that the Holy Spirit is a person and can speak, by claiming that Jehovah uses His active force like a radio transmitter. Jehovah is the sender, the holy spirit/active force is the transmitter, and the recipient is the receiver. They contend that this type of force does not go into a person and stay there, such as indwelling the person, but only has the outward effect on the body.

The Watchtower Society's governing board has also liked to use Greek or Hebrew words to drive home a point. While this may seem to make their translation correct, is it really? One thing that I can remember is the repeated explanation of the word "spirit." I won't go into all the details of the different ways they use their explanations, but I will apply it directly to the Holy Spirit. For a point of comparison I will let them speak for themselves. This is what is on the Watchtower Bible and Tract Society's online website regarding the Holy Spirit under their heading "Should You Believe the Trinity?"

> Jesus spoke of the holy spirit as a "helper," and he said it would teach, guide, and speak (John 14:16, 26; 16:13). The Greek word he used for helper (*pa ra'kle tos*) is in the masculine gender. So when Jesus referred to what the helper would do, he used masculine personal pronouns (John 16:7, 8). On the other hand, when the neuter Greek word for spirit (*pneu'ma*) is used, the neuter pronoun "it" is properly employed..... .So when the Bible uses masculine

personal pronouns in connection with *pa ra'kle tos* at
John 16: 7, 8, it is conforming to rules of grammar,
not expressing a doctrine.

It is important to understand from the entire context
of what they have on their website, that the Holy Spirit is
not a person, but just a force or thing. But let's investigate
Strong's Exhaustive Concordance to see how the Greek word
pneuma is really used in the Bible. God is a Spirit (*pneuma*)
in John 4:24. Every spirit whether it is described as evil, foul,
unclean, dumb, deaf, of infirmity, or of affliction is translated
from *pneuma,* e.g. Mark 7: 25; 9:17; Luke 13:11, plus dozens
of other times. Angels are spirits, *pneuma,* Hebrews 1:7, 14.

Here are some interesting biblical facts concerning spirits that most Christians and J.W.s are in agreement on. We
could possibly use this knowledge in a Gospel defense.

- God is a spirit being, a person-*the person.*
- Satan and the other evil and unclean spirits are
  individual spirit beings.
- The angels, whether the Archangel Michael
  (a.k.a. Jesus in their view), Gabriel, or the
  myriads of other godly angels are all individual
  beings.
- Each time they are referred to as spirit(s), it
  is translated from *pneuma.* But how often do
  Christians or J.W.s refer to any one of them as
  'it' to prove they were not beings?

So, the question is: how does the Watchtower's argument
prove that the word *pneuma* in regards to the Holy Spirit is
not a spirit being/person?

Comparison example: The New King James Version

quotes John 14:17 as: "the Spirit [*pneuma*] of truth, whom the world cannot receive, because it neither sees Him nor knows Him; but you know Him, for He dwells with you and will be in you." In contrast, the New World Translation states John 14:17 as: "the spirit [*pneuma*] of the truth, which the world cannot receive, because it neither beholds it nor knows it. YOU know it, because it remains with YOU and is in YOU."

These are just a few of the differences in their New World Translation of the Bible. My aim has been to show you why Jehovah's Witnesses will not pay any heed to what your translation of the Bible has to say if it is different from the NWT. They have to see and read what their Bible says. The only way to accomplish this is by knowing which scriptures read nearly or completely the same in both their translation and ours.

Jehovah's Witnesses' Intensive Training Program

Now we need to examine how their training program presents an obstacle to the defense of our faith. What everyone needs to realize is the reason why J.W.s are so effective in their public ministry is because t*hey have been thoroughly taught.* They know exactly what they believe, why they believe it, and the scriptures that support their beliefs. The place where they are most dangerous is where they also have been taught what the major Christian doctrines are. I must, however, clarify this. They do not know in essence what Christian doctrine is because of several factors. First, the doctrines have been twisted because no one in the Watchtower organization from the governing board down to individual Witnesses has the Holy Spirit. Secondly, everyone accepts what the governing board's early interpretation has been on the falseness of

Christian doctrines, such as the Trinity, because they have
to have implicit faith and trust in all the board's decisions.
Another reason is that the majority of people, whether they
went to church or not, don't understand the Trinity doctrine
in the first place. So when someone such as a J.W. comes
along and gives them an easy to understand explanation,
people take the bait.

Nevertheless, J.W.s do know what they have been taught
through their organization about the Christian doctrines. It
is just common sense to them that their "ministers" will be
faced with this "obstacle of false doctrine" in their ministry.
They are, therefore, prepared to rebut just about anything
someone might throw at them. If any J.W. is unable to refute
it from memory, then the other person with them might have
the answer. (This is one of the reasons there are usually two
people who come together.) If neither can immediately come
up with it, there is a reference section in the back of the New
World Translation that has the name of each Christian doctrine listed with the "appropriate" scriptures to refute it. This
tactic is very effective.

Too much emphasis cannot be placed on their training and knowledge. A common strategy in any competitive
undertaking is to learn what an opponent's game plan is. It
is then much easier to defeat them. This is a method J.W.s
have used and perfected for more than sixty years since the
1940s when they instituted their ministry training program.
The flip side is one of the main purposes of this book: to
inform as many people as possible what their game plan has
been. Then, you can defeat them at their own game by giving
a proper defense of your faith, plant seeds, and hopefully win
souls for Christ. But we must start by learning how they got
that knowledge in the first place.

A Jehovah's Witness didn't just get up one day and find

himself totally prepared for ministry. Where did the preparation come from? Fundamentally it comes from situational
training, in addition to all of the book studies. What I mean
by that statement is every J.W. who has been baptized is
required to participate in their discipleship training meetings,
although a new convert usually begins the program before
baptism. This program occurs once every week, usually on a
Thursday evening for one hour. I might add that this is not
done independently, but in front of the entire congregation
so everyone can learn from each person's presentations.

The method of operation goes like this. Each Witness
is expected/required to do a presentation at their appointed
time. Depending on how large the congregation is, this may
occur two or more times a year per person. The assignment is
the same for everyone: to create a situation or circumstance in
which a witness can be given. The person then has to create
the scenario and the dialogue to be used. The only require-
ment is that it has to be on a particular theme chosen by the
elders, which varies from student to student. (Everyone is
considered a Bible student.) Afterward, each person's method
and presentation is evaluated, recorded, and told to the student. You are privately counseled by the elder in charge of
this program on what you did well, so-so, or poorly, and on
what techniques need improvement.

Over the sixty year duration of this training program,
every possible scenario has been devised for presentation.
The scene has been depicted as taking place anywhere that
could possibly be imagined: the market, the workplace, a
family gathering, or at work in the yard. You name the place,
it's been used in a presentation.

In addition to the presenting student, he or she is
assigned a helper who plays the role of the person being wit-
nessed to. The possibilities are almost limitless. People from

every race, ethnicity, personality, etc., has been depicted. The assigned helper may be pictured as a friend, a neighbor, a family member, a co-worker, a person on the street, someone on a bus-whoever. Every possible personal problem, religious, political, or social issue has also been broached at one time or another.

The goal of all of this training is to make each witness thoroughly capable of turning *any* situation in any place into a "successful" witnessing opportunity. The most crucial facet of this ministerial program is to enable each Witness to overcome any adverse objections and/or "false teachings and scriptures" that they meet when engaged in their ministry, wherever and whenever that adversity may arise. A fitting motto for J.W.s could be, "Always be prepared."

What does the Witnesses' intensive training mean to us? It means that their knowledge and thorough training put the majority of people they make contact with at a distinct disadvantage. The reasons are really quite simple, people have not been forewarned, and frankly, Christians have definitely not been educated and spiritually prepared. Other primary reasons for J.W.s effectiveness are because people do not understand the Watchtower doctrines, why they believe them, or how to disarm them. The evangelical battlefield, so to speak, has thus far been all one-sided. The spiritual weapons that have been used boil down to these: *knowledge and control.* How many people can dispute that J.W.s don't exhibit control at the door in the vast majority of cases? *This also must change.*

You may be thinking at this stage that attempting an effective defense to a Jehovah's Witness would be very futile. But not so. Believe it or not, it is possible.

Preparations for giving a peaceable, effective Christian defense

Motives and Objectives

I believe that each person should go through an initial preparation process before we go any further in an effort to discover the motivations for wanting to know this information. Are you wanting to truly give a defense of your faith to Jehovah's Witnesses? Do you want to give glory to God? Do you really feel that you can be comfortable with doing this work? Or, is your motivation merely to prove them wrong? Do you just want to have full control over the encounters?

We must also truly acknowledge what objectives we have in giving the witness. Is the goal to plant a seed? Is the aim to spread the true gospel so that someone will hear and receive God's truth, light, knowledge, and eternal life? Or, do you want to exert control and prove them wrong for a change?

As you can see, there are various motivations and objectives that may drive a person in their activities, many more than are mentioned here. You may notice that a motivation and an objective may be one and the same thing: to exert control and prove them wrong. I can't tell you which motivations or objectives to have, or whether they may be right or wrong.

Perhaps you are wondering what my motivations and goals are. I will tell you that my motivations and objectives are any and every positive one. I tell you from my heart that my overall purpose is not to reveal or teach any information that will be used to degrade anyone in any fashion. Jesus didn't do that either. I have no bone to pick with any of the Witnesses. Neither do I have any dislike, hatred, or even any hard feelings toward any of them personally. Actually, I love those I have known as people. It is their doctrinal teaching and evangelistic methods that I find abhorrent. My intent is to show God's love, (Oh, how wonderful He is), and how it can be extended to everyone-even to Jehovah's Witnesses. Remember, after all, I used to be one of them and I know how much it hurts when someone is mean and nasty, in spite of whether I felt that I had the "real thing." And look! God had different plans for me regardless of what anyone thought or said! Well, having said that, let's go to the heart of the matter at hand.

There are several keys that must be used to prepare us in order to implement and complete a simple, effective, peaceable witness.

Recognize the Believers' Authority and Power

I believe that the most important key to Christian ministry is to look at ourselves once again and realize who we are in Christ. We are not mere humans who are working under our own power and authority. We are God's spirit children who He has given power and authority over all the powers of darkness through Christ by the Holy Spirit. This can be especially true of the deceiving spirits that are working behind the cults. The Bible clearly promises this authority and power to all believers.

We have a clear picture of Christians' power and authority when Jesus gave power and authority to seventy of His disciples to do the ministry while He was yet on earth: "Behold, I give you the authority to trample on serpents and scorpions, and over all the power of the enemy, and nothing shall by any means hurt you" (Luke 10: 19 NKJV). Jesus also promised believers that they would have a constant source of power that would be with them: "Behold, I send the Promise of My Father upon you; but tarry in the city of Jerusalem until you are endued with power on high" (Luke 24:49 NKJV). He said again at Acts 1:8: "But you shall receive power when the Holy Spirit has come upon you; and you shall be witnesses to Me in Jerusalem, and in all Judea and Samaria, and to the end of the earth" (NKJV).

Finally, Paul exhorts us to stand firm against all dark powers in Ephesians 6:10–17 since the Father has spiritually and powerfully equipped us for all good works:

> Finally, my brethren, be strong in the LORD and in the power of His might. Put on the whole armor of God, that you may be able to stand against the wiles of the devil. For we do not wrestle against flesh and blood, but against principalities, against powers, against the rulers of the darkness of this age, against spiritual hosts of wickedness in the heavenly places. Therefore take up the whole armor of God, that you

may be able to withstand in the evil day, and having done all, to stand. Stand therefore, having girded
your waist with truth, having put on the breastplate
of righteousness, and having shod your feet with the
preparation of the gospel of peace; above all, taking
the shield of faith with which you will be able to
quench all the fiery darts of the wicked one. And
take the helmet of salvation, and the sword of the
Spirit, which is the word of God.

What a promise all born-again Christians receive! So let
us prepare ourselves and increase our faith by seeking God
through prayer and studying His Word. Let us claim and use
Christ's authority by the Spirit with power, peace, love, and
confidence. It will be the confidence that we will not fall in
our gospel defense, but we will stand tall and bright as we
shed light on the world!

Keep it Simple

The second key is to keep the gospel topic and presentation
simple. The objective is to plant one seed, not an orchard.
Remember Jesus' words when He said a large tree grows from
the smallest seed. So choose the topic you want to use, but
only one. It is difficult for most people when they are new to
this area of ministry to comprehend, combine, and tackle all
of them at one time. The material has to be digested and put
into a form that is comfortable for each individual. Therefore,
it is best to work at, practice, and thoroughly know one specific topic before Jehovah's Witnesses call at your home. Your
preparation, knowledge, and confidence will result in a good
defense of your faith.

Use Scriptures

Another key is to use scriptures whenever possible. Remember, the Word of God is sharper than a two-edged sword. However, keep it simple by using only one or two scripture passages. The first reason for this simplicity is that you don't have to remember a whole list of verses. As a result, you will have more self-confidence, which will allow you to focus on the gospel message.

This is the most important reason. It bears repeating that very few scriptures in their New World Translation will read as they do in ours. So, the idea is to use the verses that are almost identical in their Bible as ours regarding words, punctuation, and capitalization. The concept is to use a power punch from their own Bible that cannot be adequately refuted. I strongly recommend you use the scriptures that I will provide below; that is unless the Spirit guides you in another direction. Amazing things can happen when the Holy Spirit is relied upon during a defense. You may be surprised at what will transpire and the scriptures that come to mind.

A third aspect of scripture usage is to have J.W.s look them up and read them from their own Bible. I know how powerful the Word of God is. Actually, I use it in a three-part way. I tell them the point about the verse I'm going to use (they hear it). Then I have them read it (they see it in their own Bible). Last, I ask them to read it out loud (they are speaking it). I have also interviewed other ex-Jehovah's Witnesses and ex-Mormons and they have the same story to tell. Almost all that I talked to had the first cord of their bondage broken as they read something from the Bible.

Take the Initiative

The third key is to take the initiative as soon as you answer
the door. If you are in doubt if they are Jehovah's Witnesses,
ask them. They won't lie. Then *you* ask the first question or
make a statement that is directly related to the *doctrine you
have chosen* to witness about. This serves to disarm them. You
know that they usually begin, carry on, and end the conversation. By using this method, you will control what topic
is talked about in a peaceable, effective way. It will not be
construed as mean or argumentative if you keep your voice
and mannerisms under control. I try to keep in mind what
I learned in a college communications course: a person can
only make you angry if you let them. Above all else, do not
let them get off onto another topic or sidetrack you with
scriptures that you have not asked about. You will understand more fully what I'm talking about a little later on as I
give examples.

"Do Not Do" Suggestions

I should also tell you a couple of don'ts. First, don't feel
intimidated or inferior in any way to a Jehovah's Witness,
other cult member, or non-Christian. You have something
much stronger than they do-you have God's Spirit in you!
They are trying to convert you, and you don't need conversion. Your mission is not only to give a defense but also to
convert them. You must remember that they have come to
your doorstep uninvited. Therefore, you have every God-
given right to direct the conversation. But, please, do it with
as much love and peace that is in you.

Here's another no-no. I don't recommend taking any of
their literature. It's not that we should be afraid of it, but of

what beneficial purpose could it possibly be to you? What does the light have in common with darkness? Take the material if you want to be assured that they will come back. Fine. It may be another opportunity to sow another seed. The chances are, though, that the same J.W. will return in a few weeks time prepared to give an argument against the point you've made. And, believe me, they will be thinking of the next visit. But that isn't what you want to accomplish. You want to make your point on the spot that will give them something to think about besides a rebuttal when they walk off your porch. I strongly suggest that you give your defense, do not take the literature, and wait for the next round of Witnesses to come.

All of this information may seem too complicated. So I will make it less confusing by giving the main points in simple steps:

1. Choose one doctrine in advance that you feel passionate about-learn it thoroughly.
2. Keep it simple.
3. Take the initiative when you answer the door. Ask if they are Jehovah's Witnesses.
4. Make a statement or ask a question right away on the topic you have chosen.
5. Use just one or two scriptures that read the same in the New World Translation.
6. Have them read it.
7. Do not let them intimidate you or change the subject. Stick to your guns. Keep them directed to your topic and your scriptures.
8. Don't take their literature. You don't need it.

Using Foreknowledge as a Spiritual Weapon

The basic thing to begin with is obtaining some basic knowledge of J.W.'s core beliefs about their God Jehovah as written in their NWT Bible that can be useful in preparing for your defense:

The Bible is the literal, indisputable Word of God-the Truth. John 17: 17 says, "Sanctify them by means of the truth, your word is truth."

Usefulness: No matter what they may say in regard to the scripture used, they have read it themselves from their own Bible. Is it the truth or not? One of their most basic beliefs is that, above all else, Jehovah hates the lie and a liar. So, the question that you may ask them is if the scriptures they've just read are the truth or not.

God is not a liar. Romans 3:4 says, "Never may that happen! But let God be found true, though every man be found a liar, even as it is written: 'That you might be proved righteous in your words and might win when you are being judged.'"

Usefulness: This is the same as above. Is God a liar or not?

Nothing God says will return to Him unfulfilled. Isaiah 55:11 says, "so my word that goes forth from my mouth will prove to be. It will not return to me without results, but it will certainly do that in which I have delighted, and it will have certain success in that for which I have sent it."

Usefulness: This is especially useful in regard to what God says about false prophets and exposing their failed predictions concerning Armageddon and Christ's coming.

God is not a God of confusion. 1 Corinthians 14:33 says, "For God is [a God], not of disorder, but of peace." (Yes, I know that it is taken from context but they use this verse very often for a variety of reasons.)

Usefulness: If a scripture in the Bible is straight forward and accurately fits the context of the passage, does God know what He's talking about or is He confused?

Effective methods
of gospel defense

There are four basic methods that you can use for a defense. These are easy and controlled, medium, challenging, and most challenging. Any defense can be used effectively based on your personality, time constraints, etc.

The format will be to give a concise statement of a Christian belief or doctrine. Then a corresponding statement regarding Jehovah's Witnesses views on the same doctrine or topic. Then I will give a general purpose of the defense followed by the appropriate scriptures that prove the Christian's stance.

In case you become curious that I do not outline all of the J.W.'s teachings and the scriptures they use as the foundation for their beliefs, it is because I believe the Spirit spoke clearly to me that this was not to be done. It could cause confusion because the Watchtower Society uses many of the same scriptures for the foundation of their beliefs and doctrines as Christians do for theirs. This would result in needing an explanation of why each and every one is wrong.

You can obtain all this information in any book on cults that include J.W.s and the Watchtower organization. The purpose of this book is to enable the reader to make a proper defense of the faith.

Here's a final reminder to always be as nice as possible; they aren't generally accustomed to being treated with tolerance and respect (it's not for their teachings but as our fellowman). This in itself serves as a weapon because it will put them at ease and hopefully get them to let their guard down.

However, *a strong note of caution:* be nice but never let your guard down and be comfortable with them! Always remember that they are not at your doorstep to talk about the weather or to make small chit-chat. *They have come with the specific purpose of converting you.*

Easy and Controlled

These methods of defense are classified as easy and controlled because they are basically one-sided, only one contains scriptures, they do not ask for any J.W. explanation, and they do not permit a two-way exchange of dialogue or ideas. They fall into the categories of Show God's Love, Witness by Mail, Personal Testimony, and Statement of Faith.

Show God's Love

- *Purpose:* to show God's love to everyone.
- *Recommended Scriptures:* None needed.
- *Statement/Questions:* Just speak the words of Jesus under the guidance of the Holy Spirit.
- *Accomplished:* Created an open door for a poor, lost,

hurting soul to enter into and receive the light and
love of Christ.

This method is the easiest one of all and can prove the
most effective. All you have to do is be nice to someone who is
associated with Jehovah's Witnesses. Don't try to avoid them.
It is only common courtesy to invite a J.W. family member or
co-worker to participate in some activity with you, the family, or group. Keep doing it, even if they turn you down every
time. You can never tell what results will come out of your
actions. Here are a couple of real-life examples of this.

When I was conducting interviews for a master's research
paper, I talked to one lady (I will call her Jenny) who was
raised in a Witness family. When Jenny grew older, she met a
non-Witness man whom she married. For people who don't
know, being "unevenly yoked" in the faith is strongly discouraged and forbidden by the Watchtower organization. While
she admitted to me that she hadn't regularly attended the
Kingdom Hall meetings for some time, she hadn't realized
that the situation regarding her marriage had escalated to
volcanic proportions. That is, until one day her sister paid
her a visit and told Jenny that she had been disfellowshipped
because of her marriage. Jenny was completely devastated and
couldn't believe that this could really be happening to her.
She was almost immediately thrown into the pits of despair
since she now felt that she was totally alienated from Jehovah
and His organization. She also felt totally alone and isolated
because nearly all of her family were Jehovah's Witnesses and
they no longer spoke to or had anything to do with her. What
hurt her most of all was that the congregation's elders had
not been to see her at all to tell her in person. She was just
disfellowshipped by a consensus of the elders and then the
decision was announced in front of the whole congregation.
Jenny knew all too well that this disfellowshiping announce-

ment didn't have to be put in extended terms because every-one automatically knew no one was to have any type of fur-ther contact with her.

Eventually, some of the elders from her Kingdom Hall did make made several visits to her home to break the news to her. She was so completely distraught, however, that she couldn't even answer the door to face them. In fact, her defense mechanism was to run into her bedroom and hide in the closet. She'd just sit there all curled up in a fetal posi-tion and cry uncontrollably. I could feel the pain that Jenny still had deep inside even after all this time had passed. But I knew there had to be a message of hope somewhere in the conclusion of her story because I had been told she was now a born-again Christian. So I asked Jenny how she overcame her anguish and what brought her into the Christian faith. I could tell that her spirit was lifted when she began to tell me of a Christian woman who was an employee at the same place where she had worked when the disfellowshipping took place. The woman had always been so nice to her. She never was stand-offish or made Jenny feel like she was different. On the contrary, the woman was always friendly and would invite Jenny to go to lunch with the girls or do something else with the group, even though Jenny usually rejected the Christian's invitations.

However, when Jenny became so desperate for someone to talk to, she thought of that Christian woman. So she went to the woman and told her all about her predicament and that she absolutely did not know what to do. Now, what was the reaction of the Christian woman? She was not demean-ing in any way, but prayed with her and comforted her the best she knew how. Then the Christian told Jenny that the best thing for her to do was to see someone who could help better her than she could. The co-worker called a Christian counselor and set up an appointment for Jenny. It was not long before this lost and hurting soul was soon on her way to spiritual recovery and true salvation.

There has been a wonderful outcome for Jenny. She and her husband have been active in the ministry for quite a few years by conducting puppet shows on Christian themes. They travel throughout their region and bring entertainment that incorporates the Gospel message for people of all ages. So you see, just being nice and showing God's love to someone can bring unexpected results. Let me give you another less dramatic but still significant example of God's love at work.

This example concerns the Jehovah's Witness lady at the Faith Mission that I told you about earlier who talked and raised questions during the Bible studies. Remember how I told you that after the Bible study we talked for an hour about doctrines, etc. Well, when we stood up to leave, I had an overwhelming compulsion come over me. I went over to that woman without even thinking about it and threw my arms around her neck, put my cheek next to hers, and gave her a great big hug! It all happened so suddenly that it took her completely by surprise. She let out an "Oh!" and put her arms around me. It was perfectly all right for me to do this. It's important to understand that I wasn't embracing a Jehovah's Witness or her false doctrines. I was embracing another human being that had, for some reason, become financially destitute, homeless, and in doubtless emotional pain. She may not remember my face or my name in the future, and I don't care. But, I am convinced that she will remember that hug. You see, I'm more than convinced that it was the Holy Spirit Who compelled me to give her that hug. Really, it wasn't even I that hugged her. It was Jesus in me. I'm also convinced that the hug was the greatest gift a person can give or receive-God's gift of love.

Witness by Mail

- *Purpose:* To give a simple yet powerful witness without any physical contact.
- *Recommended Scriptures:* The simplest is John 20:28. However, you may use any of the scriptures that are given in any of the defense scenarios throughout the book.
- *Initial Statement/Question:* Use the one that is given for whichever scenario you choose.
- *Final Comment:* Use the one given for the defense scenario you choose.
- *Accomplished:* You have taken the initiative and taken the Gospel to them.

This is a totally non-confrontational method. You can choose one of the topics presented under the medium effort section and put it in a letter or card. One venue for this method is to send a card or letter to a friend, relative, or neighbor whom you know to be a Jehovah's Witness. Please be kind and discreet because if you come across as religiously vindictive, it only serves to alienate others.

Another way is look in the yellow pages of the phone book under church listings and get the addresses for the Kingdom Halls in your area and send them a letter or card. Below is the one that I used a few weeks ago in a letter I sent to thirteen J.W. Kingdom Halls and seven to the Mormons-some of which were as far as fifty miles away. I will shortly send a card with another message. This example can be used with either religion; you just have to use the scriptures as they appear in the NWT for J.W. and the KJV for Mormons.

(To Jehovah's Witnesses)

"I understand that Jehovah's Witnesses do not believe

that Jesus is God. But John 20: 28 in your New World Translation says: 'In answer Thomas said to him: "My LORD and my God!"' This scripture plainly states that Thomas is addressing Jesus as Lord and God. If the Bible is the indisputable Word of God, is it the Truth or not?"

I didn't sign my name or give an address because with the network they have they would soon find out that I was an ex-Jehovah's Witness. Therefore, anything I send would be totally disregarded. My mission is to plant a Gospel seed of truth into whoever opens or reads the things I send. You can do whatever you want regarding your identification.

Personal Testimony

- *Purpose:* To show that God is still working in believers' lives through Jesus and by the Holy Spirit.
- *Recommended Scriptures:* None are necessary. If you want to incorporate some in your testimony, good for you.
- *Initial Statement:* I'll listen for ten minutes to what you have to say, if you'll listen for five minutes to what I have to say.
- *Final Statement:* I'm really glad you stopped by because it gave me the opportunity to share with you how God has so powerfully blessed me.
- *Accomplished:* Giving your testimony overcomes all forces of darkness regardless of whether the people at your door accept or reject what you say, because it is the blood and testimony of Christ (Based on Revelation 12:11: "And they overcame him by the blood of the Lamb and by the word of their testimony;" and Revelation 19:10: "...I am your fel-

low servant, and of your brethren who have the
testimony of Jesus. Worship God! For the spirit of
testimony of Jesus is the spirit of prophecy" NKJV).

I know that I previously said personal experiences or
testimonies were largely disregarded by J.W.s; however, they
are powerful and I have used them myself-just hoping the
person's heart is receptive. It is the Holy Spirit who knows
the heart and can truly plant it and make it grow. We just put
it out there for Him to work with. The following method is
the one I use, as well as some church pastors I know.

When you find that Jehovah's Witnesses (this also works
with Mormons) are at the door, you simply say that you will
listen to them on one condition: They may have ten minutes
to say whatever they have to say, *then*, they will have to listen
to what you say for five minutes. *But*, when you are finished
there will be no discussion. If they agree, then hold them to
it. If you have a watch on, just give them the allotted time
and then they are done. You also keep your end of the bargain
for the time period you have set for yourself. If they try to
carry on when you are finished, just tell them an agreement
was made and you don't have any more time-it is finished.

Statement of Faith

- *Purpose:* To shed light on true Christian doctrine.
- *Recommended Scriptures:* None necessary.
- *Initial Statement:* I don't have the time for a discussion today, but I'll quickly tell you what I believe.
- *Final Statement:* This is what the Bible teaches, and that is what I believe.
- *Accomplished:* A non-confrontational, peaceable witness for the pure Gospel.

This particular method is also easy and controlled, but it is harder if you do not know exactly what you believe. However, you do not have to listen to anything they say. You just make a statement of your belief. You have no discussion. The following is an example of what you could say-again, it's up to you to pick and choose all or part of it. Be creative and adapt it to yourself, just keep it biblical and factual.

When they come to your door and you find out who they are, you just say you don't have time for a discussion but you will quickly tell them what you believe. Use any of those you wish from the following list.

- I believe that there is one Almighty God that is a Triune God made up of God the Father, God the Son, and God the Holy Spirit.
- I believe that each the Father, the Son, and the Holy Spirit-as God-are all-knowing, all-powerful, and ever-present in all places.
- I believe that God had a plan for mankind's salvation to save us from sin and death.
- I believe that this plan began to be fulfilled when God the Son was conceived by the Virgin Mary when the Holy Spirit overshadowed Mary.
- I believe that Jesus taught and preached the Kingdom of God, and He laid the foundation of His church while on earth.
- I believe that Jesus' mission was fulfilled when He suffered, died, was bodily resurrected, and ascended into heaven.
- Because of Jesus' sacrifice, I believe that when I accepted Him as my Lord, my God, and my Savior, that I was born again of the Spirit,

redeemed, sanctified, and justified as a child of God.

- I believe God's promise that I will live for eternity with Jesus in heaven.

Excuse yourself by saying that this is all the time that you have right now. Glad you stopped by. This can be longer, shorter, or you may want to add something different about what you believe. It's all up to you. This is just a list of general, concise Christian statements of faith. Overall, you will have achieved a statement of your faith, given a defense of the Gospel, sown seeds, set the tone of the encounter, and you had no discussion or argument. Mission accomplished!

Medium Effort Defense

This defense method is what I consider a medium effort because it combines three components: the basic Christian doctrine, which is the foundation for each defense; what the Jehovah's Witnesses belief(s) is concerning the topic; and you also need to know the one or two scripture references that apply to the topic. I might stress that you need to be acquainted with the verses you choose; however, you do not need to memorize them in their entirety. Just remember the book, chapter, and verse. These topics include Jesus is God and The Holy Spirit.

*** Important: Every opening statement in each defense must be worded carefully. The main point will be shown by the asterisks. Everything else is built on it. For instance, if they want to sidetrack you into their direction, use elements of the opening statement or question to draw them back into your chosen topic. The conclusion is also based on the beginning.

Jesus is God

Christian Doctrine:

It is all about Jesus! Much of this material was incorporated into the faith statement that was in the easy and controlled defense method. It is given again so that any information needed for any defense is in its right place without having to leaf through the book.

Christians' core belief is that Jesus is the second person of the triune God. He has all the qualities of God since He is all-knowing, all-powerful, and ever-present. He existed in the heavens as God the Word, but was supernaturally incarnated as a human through the virgin birth. This was accomplished by means of the Holy Spirit as He over-shadowed Mary. His earthly mission and purpose was to preach the truth of God, establish His church, suffer, die, and be resurrected as a means of redeeming mankind from sin and death and giving them everlasting life.

Hebrews 2:17–18 also tells us why Jesus took on flesh, "Therefore, in all things He had to be made like His brethren, that He might be a merciful and faithful High Priest in things pertaining to God, to make propitiation for the sins of the people. For in that He Himself has suffered, being tempted, He is able to aid those who are tempted." Therefore, Jesus having successfully completed His mission and purpose, has provided all people the opportunity to receive forgiveness of sins, the guarantee of the Holy Spirit to seal us, and a resurrection to eternal heavenly life-through God's love, grace, and mercy.

Jehovah's Witness Doctrine on Jesus:

J.W.s believe that Jesus was never any part of God but was the firstborn of all creation—the Archangel Michael. Since he was the first creation, God bestowed on him the privilege and power to help Jehovah to create everything else in heaven and earth. As the Archangel Michael, he is head of all the other angels. As an angel he never had, nor does he now have, any rightful claim to deification. They do say, however, that Jesus is divine because the Bible makes it clear that he had a divine nature. Nevertheless, they claim he has never been all-knowing, all-powerful, or ever-present.

They also believe that Michael's spirit life was transferred into the womb of Mary by Jehovah's spirit power (not the Holy Spirit). He was given the name Jesus when he was born as a human. Although Jesus had a perfect human body and did not sin, Jesus was purely human with no godly attributes or power with the exception of those he performed after he was anointed with Jehovah's spirit following his baptism. Absolute perfection in body and living was necessary for Jesus to provide the perfect physical sacrifice to replace the one lost by the perfect man, Adam, because of his sin and rebellion. Thus, J.W.s claim that Jesus could only refer to Himself as "a god," as they have translated the passage in John 1:1 of the New World Translation of the Holy Scriptures.

They also believe that Jesus as a man taught the truth of God's Word, suffered, died, and was resurrected. His resurrection was not a physical one, though, but one with a spiritual body that he could materialize at will. They also believe that Jesus ascended into heaven, but returned to His pre-human existence as the Archangel Michael who stands at the right hand of God. Michael, in their belief, received his kingly power and authority in heaven in 1914 when Jehovah established his heavenly kingdom. Jesus/Michael will only keep this position until He leads the heavenly army at Armageddon, then he will give all power back to Jehovah. He will then just be the head of the angels again.

Scenario #1

- *Purpose:* To show that Jesus is God.
- *Recommended scripture:* John 20: 28.
- *Scripture comparison:* The NKJV quotes John 20:28 as: "And Thomas answered and said to Him, 'My LORD and my God!'" The NWT translation states John 20:28 as: "In answer Thomas said to him: 'My LORD and my God!'" As you can see, both translations are almost identical in their entirety, but exactly the same in the phrase, "My LORD and my God!" This verse is almost exactly the same in all the Bible translations that I have examined. This verse has been the foundation stone, so to speak, of many ex-Jehovah's Witnesses believing in the deity of Jesus, myself included! There is really no valid argument that can dispute what this scripture says, not even if the Society's official stance on this verse is that Jesus can be addressed as "God" because He has a divine nature. No other scriptures are needed. I might add that many Witnesses are not aware of this verse and the Society's official stance on it. I had never taken notice of it for twenty years.
- *Initial Statement/Question:* "I base all the religious messages someone brings me on what they believe about Jesus. Do you believe Jesus is God?"
- *Final Statement:* I can't accept your message because it's a different gospel than what the Bible teaches. (This is based on Galatians 1:7, 8: "...but there are some who trouble you and want to pervert the gospel of Christ. But even if we, or an angel from heaven, preach any other gospel to you than what

we have preached to you, let him be accursed."
NKJV).

What I'm going to do in this scenario is give you the exact encounter I had just a couple of weeks ago when two Mormons came to my door. This verse, this defense, works equally well with both Jehovah's Witnesses and Mormons. (Mormons believe Jesus was a pre-existent spirit who was transferred by sexual intercourse between Father God and Mary into a human body to prove himself. He consequently became an exalted man by righteous works and he ultimately became a god after death—but was not the one and only supreme God.) The only difference is that Mormons use the King James Version of the Bible. This is a prime example of everything that I have been telling you about.

I answered the door one afternoon, and there were two young men on my porch. Since they were dressed in black trousers and white shirts, I assumed they were Mormons. I didn't invite them in but went out onto the porch. The following details unfolded.

Mormon #1: "Good afternoon, how are you today?"
Me: "I'm doing very good, blessed."

(They started their presentation but I stopped them. Just as I told you regarding J.W.s, here is where knowledge of their belief system and methods helped, specifically knowing they believed Jesus is "a god." I also knew that the Mormons' usual method of drawing people into agreement and conversation with them is using Jesus as a starting point. They ask, "You believe in Jesus, don't you?")
Me: "I have to tell you that I always base a religious message

by what it says about Jesus. ***Do you believe Jesus is God?" (Opening statement and question)

Mormon # 2: "We believe he is 'a god'."

Me: "No, not 'a god.' Do you believe that Jesus is God?" (Bringing them back to my question.)

Mormon #2: "We believe that Jesus is the Son of God."

Me: "No, not the Son of God. Do you believe Jesus is God?" (Brought them back to my question.)

At this point they stuck in more of their thoughts and repeated what they had already said, but more or less hemmed and hawed.

Me: "Well, I believe that the Bible tells us He is God. I don't have my Bible handy, but I'm sure you have a Bible with you."

Mormon #1: "Yes, but we only use the King James Version." (I directed them to their own Bible version)

Me: "That's all right. I believe it will read the same. Would you look up and read John 20:28?" (I acted as a guide for them to see it in their own Bible.)

So Mormon #1 finds the passage and stands there reading it to himself.

Me: "Would you read to me what it says?" (They are speaking it.)

Mormon #1 read it, but made no comment.

Me: "That says Thomas was calling Jesus both Lord and God. It has the capitals 'L' and 'G' denoting deity-that Jesus was God."

Mormon #2: "Oh, that was probably just an expression Thomas used because he was so overwhelmed." (Like J.W.s, this is where two people are advantageous. #2 came in with a comment when #1 didn't know what to say.)

Me: "No, that wasn't just an expression. All you have to do is

go back to verse 27 and you see that he was addressing
Jesus. And that's exactly what the Bible says-Thomas
answered Him-Jesus. Thomas was talking directly to
Him and referring to Jesus as Lord and God, not mak-
ing an expression." (I used knowledge of the whole
Biblical sequence to prove the point.)

This is just an extract of the entire conversation, but
these exact words were exchanged regarding Jesus. We con-
tinued for an hour or more, by God's grace, until we had
covered several more doctrines. But they never could give a
biblical or non-biblical rebuttal of that verse or anything else
we talked about.

The encounter was concluded when I made three definite statements. One was that I couldn't accept their message
because it was a different gospel than what the Bible teaches.
I made the second statement that I was solid in my faith and
they were not to mistake my willingness to talk with them
as interest because I was aware they were at my door to persuade me to their way of thinking; and I let them know that
was precisely my mission in talking to them. (This was not
out of rudeness, but in response to their persistence in trying
to get me to agree to let them come back for more visits.)
The third statement was that I really had no more time to
talk because I had to finish supper because my husband likes
to eat when he comes home from work. (They appreciate the
wife's care of husband.)

What I accomplished was a defense of the Gospel; I took
charge of the encounter by choosing the doctrine topic, and
I used the verse that I knew could not be effectively refuted.
I could also be effective by knowing basic Mormon beliefs
and witnessing methods. No matter what they said, I did not
let them off the hook by letting them give me an answer to a
question that I wasn't asking about. I must tell you an amus-

ing part of the encounter. When they saw that I couldn't be moved, they asked me if my husband was as strong in his belief as I was in mine! *See!* This is a perfect example of how the Mormons and J.W.s both think. If they don't get one, they'll try to get the other!

A crucial bit of information I want you to know is that never once during that encounter did I get angry, argumentative, raise my voice, use a sarcastic tone or language, nor did I try to intentionally offend them. But, I was pretty hard on them because I didn't compromise my faith or God's Word one bit. I was satisfied. My goal was accomplished!

After they left, my husband and I sat down at the table to eat supper, and I felt so good, so thankful! I just had to say, "Thank you, God! Praise you, God! Thank you for the opportunity I had to speak the truth of your Word today to these people." And I meant every word of what I said. It was and is a privilege and a blessing to me.

Jesus is God Number Two

- *Purpose:* To show that Jesus is God by the titles they both share.
- *Recommended Scriptures:* Revelations 1:8 and Revelation 22:12–13.
- *Scripture comparisons:* Revelation 1:8 *a notable feature of this scripture is God the Almighty is being quoted as the speaker.* The New King James Version quotes Revelation 1:8 as: "I am the Alpha and the Omega, the Beginning and the End, says the LORD, who is and who was and who is to come, the Almighty." The New World Translation states Revelation 1:8 as: "I am the Alpha and the Omega," says Jehovah God, "the One who is and who was and who is

coming, the Almighty." As you can see both translations have God Almighty saying He is the Alpha
and Omega; significantly the NWT uses the words
"Jehovah God," which is important because then
there can be no doubt in their minds about who is
speaking here.

Revelations 22:12–13 *a notable feature of this
scripture is that it is indisputable that Jesus is speaking.* The New King James Version quotes this verse
as: "And behold, I am coming quickly, and My
reward is with Me, to give to every one according
to his work. I am the Alpha and the Omega, the
Beginning and the End, the First and the Last."
The New World Translation says of these same
verses: "Look! I am coming quickly, and the reward
I give is with me, to render to each one as his work
is. I am the Alpha and the Omega, the first and the
last, the beginning and the end."

- *Initial Statement/Question:* "I've heard that
Jehovah's Witnesses do not believe Jesus is God. Is
that true?"
- *Final Question:* "Would Jehovah allow Jesus or
anyone else to assume the same titles for himself
unless He was equal to God?"
- *Final Statement:* "I can't accept your message
because it is a different gospel than what the Bible
teaches."
- *Accomplished:* You have shown that Jesus is God by
title and rank. This is an especially strong defense
because of the New World Translation's rendition
of the verses you use in this encounter. The scriptures used prove that Almighty God is the same as
Jesus because the titles attributed to each one are

exactly the same in these verses. The most important point is that Jesus calls Himself the Alpha and
the Omega.

The NWT drives home the point for you in
Revelation 1 by actually using "Jehovah God."
Then in Revelation 22, Jesus confirms that He is
God, not just by stating "I am the Alpha and the
Omega," but makes it emphatic by giving all defi-
nitions of the words. It is significant that all three
are used because it signifies that God is making a
definite point.

Scenario #2

Once you ask them if they are Jehovah's Witnesses just say:

You: "I don't have time for a lot of discussion, but I'm glad
you stopped by. I have a question that I'd like to ask you.
***I've heard that you don't believe Jehovah and Jesus are
both God. ***Do you believe Jesus is God? I'd appreciate
it if you keep it brief with a simple yes or no answer."

J.W.: "No."

You: "Well, one of the reasons I believe Jesus is God is based
on what is written in Revelation. I see you have a Bible
there, would you please read Revelation 1:8?" (Make
sure they don't just read it to themselves, but out loud.)
"It says there that Jehovah God is calling Himself the
Alpha and the Omega, and He is coming. Now, the reason I believe Jesus is God is in Revelation 22:12–13.
Would you please read that?

You: "There's no doubt that Jesus was talking in this passage and calls Himself the Alpha and Omega just as
Jehovah says of Himself. ***Would Jehovah allow Jesus,

or anyone else, to assume the same titles for Himself unless He was equal to God? I believe that there are only two conclusions that can be made from these passages. Either the Bible is the truth and Jesus was making Himself equal with God. Or, Jesus, who is the Word, is guilty of blasphemy. I can't speak for you, but I don't-I can't-believe that. I don't want to be rude, but I don't have any more time to talk. Thanks for stopping by."

Scenario #3

- *Purpose:* To show that the Lord God and Jesus are both the same God by performing the same action.
- *Recommended Scriptures:* Revelation 22:6 and Revelation 22:16.
- *Scripture comparisons:* The New King James Version quotes Revelation 22:6 as: "Then he said to me, 'These words are faithful and true.' And the LORD God of the holy prophets sent His angel to show His servants the things which must shortly take place." The New World Translation states this verse as: "And he said to me: 'These words are faithful and true;' yes, Jehovah the God of the inspired expressions of the prophets sent his angel forth to show his slaves the things that must shortly take place."
- The New King James Version quotes Revelation 22:16 as: "'I, Jesus, have sent My angel to testify to you these things in the churches...'" The New World Translation states Revelation 22:16 as: "'I Jesus, sent my angel to bear witness to YOU people of these things for the congregations...'"

- *Initial Statement:* "I've heard that Jehovah's Witnesses do not believe Jesus is God. Is that true?"
- *Final Statements:* "The Bible is the whole truth and it says that Jehovah sent the angel and Jesus sent the angel. This clearly proves that Jesus is God. I cannot accept your message because it is a different gospel than what the Bible teaches."
- *Accomplished:* You have shown that the Bible plainly states that God and Jesus performed the same action, sending the angel; bottom line is you have shown Jesus is God.

You can see that Watchtower Society's New World Translation makes the contrast parallel even better than the New King James Version. They actually use "Jehovah the God" in Revelation 22:6, which shows He sent the angel with the message. Then Jesus applies the same action to Himself in Revelation 22:16. The conclusion has got to be either the Bible is the truth or it isn't; Jesus is part of the triune God or He isn't. It can't be both ways. You can use the exact same scenario structure as that the one used in scenario number two, except use the different final statement.

Jesus Cannot be the Archangel Michael

I will only give a very brief explanation of both the Christian and J.W. doctrines on Jesus since this material has already been covered in previous sections. This will just serve as a memory prod.

Christians believe that Jesus is the second person of the triune God and was known as the Word. He was incarnated into Mary's womb by the Holy Spirit and was born as Jesus in the flesh. He was, however, fully human and fully God. During His ministry, He preached, taught, performed miracles, suffered, died by crucifixion, was resurrected, and finally ascended into heaven. He always was, is, and will be God who is all-knowing, all-powerful, and ever-present.

Jehovah's Witnesses believe that Jesus is not God. Jesus was the first creation of Jehovah and was known as the Archangel Michael in His pre-human existence. They believe that God transplanted Michael's life spirit by means of His power into Mary's womb. Michael's life force developed and was born as a human and was given the name Jesus. They also believe that Jesus was purely human with a divine nature, but had/has no godly attributes such as omniscient power and knowledge or ever-presence. J.W.s teach that once Jesus died and was resurrected with a spiritual body, that He ascended into heaven but was transformed back into the Archangel Michael.

Scenario #1

- *Purpose:* To show that Jesus was not the incarnate Archangel Michael.
- *Recommended scriptures:* Hebrews 1:12; Hebrews 13:8
- *Scripture comparisons:* The New King James Version quotes Hebrews 1:12 as: "...And they will be changed, But You are the same and Your years will not fail." Similarly, the New World Translation states Hebrews 1:12 as: "...and they will be changed, but you are the same and your years will never run out." The New King James Version quotes Hebrews 13: 8 as: "Jesus Christ is the same yesterday, today, and forever." Similarly,

the New World Translation states Hebrews 13:8 as: "Jesus Christ is the same yesterday and today, and forever."

- *Initial Statement/Question:* "I've been told that J.W.s believe that Jesus was and is now the Archangel Michael. Yes or no, is that true?"
- *Final Statement:* I believe that who Jesus was thousands of years ago is who He is today and forever.
- *Conclusion:* "I can't receive your message because it is a different gospel than what the Bible teaches."
- *Accomplished:* You have defeated them with their own belief system.

You: *** "I've been told that Jehovah's Witnesses believe that the Archangel Michael was born as Jesus, then when He was taken back into heaven, He is Michael again. Yes or no, is that true?" (Don't let them get started on their explanations.) "I'm going to have to disagree with you because of what the Bible says.

"Would you please look up Hebrews 1:12 and read it to me? That verse says that Jesus will be the same forever. Since you have the book of Hebrews open, would you look up and read chapter 13:8? See, that also says that Jesus is always the same. Jesus never changes. What Jesus was thousands of years ago is what He is today, and will always be-the same forever. So I can't receive your message because it is a different gospel than what the Bible teaches."

If you are game for it, you can enter into a discussion on it. You will be hit with 1 Thessalonians 4:16 and Jude 9. The former says in paraphrasing that Jesus will make His return with a loud shout, and "with the voice of an archangel..." Jude says that Michael disputed with Satan over Moses' body. If you get into this discussion, ask this question: "Can you show me one, just one, scripture in either the Old or New Testament that plainly says in black and white that Jesus was, is, or ever will be the Archangel Michael?" They can't do it. It isn't there. You don't even have to make any argument that Jesus is God. The goal is to get them to start thinking for themselves-one seed at a time.

Holy Spirit

Christian Doctrine:

Christians believe that the Holy Spirit is a spirit person and the third person of the triune God. As such, He is equal with and has all the power attributes of the Father and Son. He is all-powerful, all-knowing, and present everywhere at all times. As a person, He has a mind, sees, hears, bears witness, directs, leads, comforts, guides, teaches, and indwells the believer.

Jehovah's Witness Doctrine:

A simple recap of their belief about the Holy Spirit:

1. The Holy Spirit is not a person, let alone part of the triune God.
2. It is not all-knowing, all-powerful, nor present everywhere at all times.
3. The spirit spoken of in scripture is God's active force or power, like lightning.
4. The spiritual work gifts were given to first century believers only.
5. All tales of supernatural works in our lives are the work of Satan since he has power to perform signs and wonders.

The most basic thing to keep in mind is that J.W.s believe

that the Holy Spirit is not God. He is not even a being and does not indwell any believer. The spirit descends and rests on a person just as the spirit descended on Jesus in the form of a dove after His baptism.

Scenario #1

- *Purpose:* To show that the Holy Spirit is not an impersonal force or power, but a real Being with Godlike power and abilities. Even though I stated earlier the Watchtower's official explanation of this verse, you might nevertheless get someone who is in doubt, new, or just doesn't know about it. You never know how God will work. In any event, rejoice! I say again, rejoice, because you have spoken the truth.
- *Recommended Scripture:* John 16: 13,14
- *Scripture comparison:* The New King James Version quotes John 16:13, 14 as: "However, when He, the Spirit of truth, has come, *He will guide* you into all truth; for *He will not speak* on His own authority, but whatever *He hears, He will speak; and He will tell you things to come.* He will glorify Me, for *He will take* of what is Mine *and declare it* to you." The New World Translation states John 16:13,14 as: "However, when that one arrives, the spirit of the truth, *he will guide YOU* into all the truth, for *he will not speak* of his own impulse, but *what things he hears he will speak,* and *he will declare to YOU the things coming.* That one will glorify me, because *he will receive* from what is mine *and will declare* it to YOU."
- *Initial Statement/Question:* Is it true that J.W.s

believe that the Holy Spirit is not a person but just God's power like lightning? Yes or no, is that true?

- *Final Statements:* We can see that the Bible says that the Holy Spirit not only does everything that a person does, but has God's power and authority. If that's what Jesus said and it's in the Bible, that's what I believe.

- *Accomplished:* You have accomplished three things: First, you have let them know you have some knowledge of their beliefs. Second, you have chosen the topic and posed the question. Third, you have controlled the conversation.

You answer the door and don't know who it is.

J. W: "Hello, how are you today? We are in the neighborhood today making Christian calls." (There are no set introductions of themselves or clear-cut statements of purpose so this could vary.)

You: "Are you Jehovah's Witnesses?" (You have identified them but more importantly stopped their presentation.)

J. W: "Yes."

You: "Well, I only have a few minutes to spare today, but there is a question I have for you about something. ***Is it true that you believe that the Holy Spirit is not a person but just God's power, like lightning? Could you just give me a yes or no answer?"

You: "I don't really understand this at all. I see that you have a Bible with you. Would you please read John 16: 13 and 14?"

***Important: do not ask them to explain what they've read. By doing this, you have chosen the verse to support God's Word, your belief, and deprived them of giving verses to support their doctrine. Again, the ball remains in your court. When they have finished reading the verse, you will now make a statement-not a question:

You: "That's exactly how my Bible reads. We can see that the Holy Spirit not only does everything that a person does, but has God's power and authority. (You may say something like this: Jesus referred to the Holy Spirit by using the word "he," as well as saying the Spirit can speak, hear, foretell events, teach the knowledge of God, and gives Jesus' power and authority to people just like a real person.) If that is what Jesus said and it's in the Bible, that is what I believe."

If they try to come back with something else just respond with, "I don't have time to discuss this any further with you. But I just have to say that I believe that the Bible is the indisputable Word of God, and God is not a liar. I really do have to go. Thanks for stopping by."

Your argument should at least be mildly convincing to them because you have used their own core beliefs that the Bible is the indisputable Word of God and God cannot lie. If an objection is made regarding the Greek words *parakletos* and *pneuma* and you decide to continue the conversation, tell them that God, Satan, demons, and God's angels are all individual spirit beings. In fact, they are so as translated from the Greek word *pneuma*. This most likely will not come up unless you happen to have an elder or very skilled Witness at your door. This information was presented in the section of why scriptures do not work with them. Scriptures to use in upholding this stance are John 4:24; Mark 7:25; 9:7; Luke 13:11; and Hebrews 1:7, 14.

Scenario #2

- *Purpose:* To show that Jesus not only told the apostles what the Holy Spirit would do, but that the Holy Spirit actually performed the acts Jesus said He would.
- *Recommended Scriptures:* John 16:13, 14; Acts 10:19,20
- *Scripture comparisons:* The New King James Version quotes John 16: 13–14 as: "However, when He, the Spirit of Truth, has come, He will guide you into all truth; for He will not speak on His own authority, but whatever He hears He will speak; and He will tell you things to come. He will glorify Me, for He will take of what is Mine and declare it to you." Similarly, the New World Translation states John 16:13–14 as: "However when that one arrives, the spirit of the truth, he will guide YOU into all the truth, for he will not speak of his own impulse, but what things he hears he will speak, and he will declare to YOU the things coming. That one will glorify me, because he will receive from what is mine and will declare it to *YOU*." The New King James Version quotes Acts 10:19–20 as: "While Peter thought about the vision, the *Spirit said to him,* 'Behold, three men are seeking you. *Arise therefore, go down and go with them,* doubting nothing; *for I have sent them.*'" Similarly, the New World Translation states Acts 10:19–20 as: "As Peter was going over in his mind about the vision, the spirit said: "Look! Three men are seeking you. However, rise, go downstairs and be on your way with them, not doubting at all, because I have dispatched them."

These scripture passages are also forthright, for they show the Spirit speaking, directing, and commanding. Is that God-like power or what?

You may proceed as I suggested in scenario one, except after they read John 16:13–4 you may say: "Now, I not only believe that Jesus said the Holy Spirit could and would do these things but the Bible also tells us says that the Spirit actually did these things in Acts 10:19–20. Would you please read that?"

After they read it, tell them you have to believe what the Bible says: that the Holy Spirit is not a force like lightning but a real being with God-like qualities and abilities. Conclude as in scenario one.

It is entirely up to how you feel the Holy Spirit is leading you as to how you proceed. Regardless of which way you go, you have to remember to keep them focused on what you have to say. The reason is that the longer the conversation goes on the more likely it is that they will try to make a defense for their doctrine by giving explanations using support sources other than scriptures. This could lead in another direction entirely. Therefore, it is better to make it as brief as possible until you get more experience, comfort, and confidence.

Scenario #3

- *Purpose:* to show that the Holy Spirit dwells within the believer. Additional thoughts based on logic: How can the Holy Spirit not be everywhere if He indwells more than one person at a time-one person may be in China, another person in South America, another one in Greenland? This could be effective because they believe that Jehovah's spirit is on members of the 144,000—8,000 of which

they claimed were living throughout the earth in
2005.

- *Recommended Scriptures:* Romans 8:11; 1
  Corinthians 3:16
- *Scripture comparisons:* The New King James
  Version quotes Romans 8:11 as: "But if the Spirit
  of Him who raised Jesus from the dead dwells in
  you, He who raised Christ from the dead will also
  give life to your mortal bodies through His Spirit
  who dwells in you." Similarly, the New World
  Translation states Romans 8:11 as: "If, now, the
  spirit of him that raised up Jesus from the dead
  dwells in *YOU*, he that raised up Christ Jesus from
  the dead will also make *YOUR* mortal bodies alive
  through his spirit that resides in *YOU*." The New
  King James Version quotes 1 Corinthians 3:16
  as: "Do you not know that you are the temple of
  God and that the Spirit of God dwells in you?"
  Similarly, the New World Translation quotes 1
  Corinthians 3:16 as: "Do *YOU* not know that *YOU*
  people are God's temple, and that the spirit of God
  dwells in *YOU*?"
- *Initial Statement/Question:* I have to base religious
  messages on whether they conform to the Bible.
  Is it true that J.W.s believe the Holy Spirit is just
  a force like lightning and not everywhere at the
  same time?
- *Final Statement:* That's why I believe the Holy
  Spirit dwells inside every believer, because the
  Bible says so.

You make a statement once you find out they're J.W.s: ***
"I have to base religious messages on whether they conform

to the Bible. ***Is it true that you believe that the Holy Spirit is just a force and is not everywhere at the same time? Just a simple yes or no would be appreciated. I don't believe that the Bible teaches that, especially in Romans 8:11. Would you look that up, please?"

After it's read: "See, that clearly says that the Spirit resides in the believer. Now would you look up 1 Corinthians 3:16, please?"

After that's read: "Now that's why I believe that the Holy Spirit dwells inside every believer-because the Bible says so. I believe that He has to be everywhere, too, because one person the Spirit dwells in may be on one side of the world, while another person who is indwelt is on the other side of the earth. You know, I've really enjoyed talking to you, but I really don't have any more time to continue this discussion. Thanks for stopping by."

Challenging Defense

These defense topics are more challenging because they require knowing more Christian doctrines, more scriptures, and a broader knowledge of Jehovah's Witnesses' more complex doctrines. They not only serve to give a defense of the Gospel but also expose their doctrines as false. Therefore, more time is needed to prepare.

False Prophet

Christian and Watchtower beliefs on the battle of Armageddon must be examined since it is the core of this defense.

Christian Belief on Armageddon:

Although there are varying views on whether Armageddon is to be a spiritual or literal battle, nearly all Christians believe that it is an event that will take place at an unknown hour. Jesus made it abundantly clear in Matthew 24: 36 that no one in heaven or on earth would ever know when this is to occur-only Father God. Thus, when anyone proposes to have a revelation, special knowledge, or a correct timetable or calculation for an exact date for Armageddon, the vast majority of true Christians can safely ignore the prediction.

Jehovah's Witness on Armageddon:

J.W.s believe that Armageddon is a literal earthly battle between the Archangel Michael, a.k.a. Jesus, with his heavenly army and all the earthly nations under the forces of evil. Armageddon will do away with all non-Jehovah's Witness people, as well as all the nations and all the social, religious, and governmental structures throughout the entire earth. Nevertheless, the earth as a planet will not be destroyed. They believe that there will be Jehovah's Witnesses who will come out of the great tribulation and Armageddon alive and will continue living on the earth.

Important Factors to Know

Several sects and/or cults have made various predictions for over 150 years regarding the coming of the Lord and Armageddon and none of them have occurred. This is especially true of the Watchtower Society who has predicted that Armageddon would occur in a specific year at least three times. Two of these predictions, for instance, were to occur in or close to the years 1914 and 1974. They made these claims years in advance of those dates. I know for a fact that around 1970, they first advanced the declaration that Armageddon would definitely occur in or close to 1974.

In addition to these predictions, they also claimed that the old time prophets would return to planet earth to a certain place in California in the 1920s. In order to have a proper place for them, an elaborate home was built to house not only the great prophets but the high-ranking members of the Watchtower Society. Needless to say, this didn't happen either.

The Watchtower organization claims that they can do this because they are not giving the specific month, day, or hour. Whenever their predictions do not happen in the years they say, the assertion is that they made wrong calculations, or they will be happening shortly. When they are faced with the failure of them to occur at all, they say that they have not prophesied but predicted. We shall soon see if there is a difference by examining the following facts.

1. God says: "And if you say in your heart, '*How shall we know the word which the* LORD *has not spoken?'—when a prophet speaks in the name of the* LORD, *if the thing does not happen or come to pass, that is the thing which the* LORD *has not spoken; the prophet has spoken it presumptuously; you shall not be afraid of him*" (Deuteronomy 18:21- 22 NKJV).

2. The Watchtower Bible and Tract Society claims to be the *only authentic religious organization recognized by God.*

3. They claim that God reveals His truthful knowledge and His will *to that organization only.*

4. God *speaks* through that organization only.

5. When the Watchtower Society announces the approach of Armageddon, they claim they are *not prophesying but making a prediction.*

6. The New American Webster College Dictionary's definitions: "Prophet 1. One who predicts 2. A spokesman, esp. one inspired by God." "Prophesy-predict, foretell;" "Prophecy-a prediction of the future;" "Predict-foretell, prophesy."

Now let's consider all of the information contained in the knowledge factors presented here and come to a logical conclusion. First, the scriptural evidence reveals that God's inspired word or message through a spokesman or prophet will always come true. According to the Watchtower Society they, and only they, are God's inspired instrument to dispense the proper food (knowledge) for Him and to speak God's word and will to all people at this time (a prophet/spokesman). Working in that capacity, several times they have warned people years in advance of God's coming wrath at Armageddon, which was to occur in a specific year (prophecy/prediction). These predictions have not come true. The first conclusion is the Watchtower Society is not God's prophet or spokesman. The final conclusion: *The Watchtower Society is a false prophet.*

Note: If you choose to use this topic, it might be a good idea to have a dictionary with the words and definitions cited above marked in some way. This is just in case you want to use it if they come up with the prediction/prophecy argument.

Scenario for False Prophet

- *Purpose:* To tactfully expose the Watchtower Society as a false prophet regarding their repeated predictions that Armageddon would *definitely* occur in or around specific years. 1.) To reveal that anyone who makes a prophecy/prediction in God's name that does not take place is not from God, i.e., their organization's numerous predictions that Armageddon will take place at specific times. 2.) To *get them to actually think for themselves* about these false predictions and the repercussions that have to be faced for adhering to the teachers that promote them.

- *Recommended Scriptures:* Isaiah 55:11; Deuteronomy 18:21,22; 2 Peter 2:1
- *Scripture comparisons:* The new King James Version quotes Isaiah 55:11 as: "So shall My word be that goes forth from My mouth; It shall not return to Me void, But it shall accomplish what I please, And it shall prosper in the thing for which I sent it." Similarly, the New World Translation states Isaiah 55:11 as: "so my word that goes forth from my mouth will prove to be. It will not return to me without results, but it will certainly do that in which I have delighted, and it will have certain success in that for which I have sent it."

The New King James Version quotes Deuteronomy 18:21–22 as: "And if you say in your heart, 'How shall we know the word which the LORD has not spoken?'—when a prophet speaks in the name of the LORD, if the thing does not happen or come to pass, that is the thing which the LORD has not spoken; the prophet has spoken it presumptuously; you shall not be afraid of him.'" Similarly, the New World Translation states Deuteronomy 18:21–22 as: "And in case you should say in your heart: '*How shall we know the word that Jehovah has not spoken?*' when the *prophet speaks in the name of Jehovah and the word does not occur or come true, that is the word that Jehovah did not speak.* With presumptuousness the prophet spoke it. *You must not get frightened at him.*"

The New King James Version quotes 2 Peter 2:1 as: "But there were also false prophets among the people, even as there will be false teachers among you, who will secretly bring in destructive heresies, even denying the LORD who bought them, and bring on themselves swift destruction." Similarly, the New World Translation states of 2 Peter 2:1 as: "However, there also came to be false prophets among the people, as there will also be false teachers among *YOU*. These very ones will quietly bring in destructive sects and will disown even the owner that bought them, bringing speedy destruction upon themselves."

- *Initial Statement/Question:* "I take the Bible's warning seriously that there will be false teachers in the last days. Do you agree with what Isaiah 55:11 says?"
- *Accomplished:* You have shown them in plain, bold facts that the Watchtower is not God's spokesman. The organization is a false prophet.

You answer the door and the person tells you they are making Christian calls in the area.

You: "Are you J.W.s?"
J.W.: "Yes."
You: *** "Well, I have to tell you that I seriously take the Bible's warning in 2 Peter 2: 1, that there will be false teachers in the last days. So I base the truth of any mes-

sage on whether it measures up to what God's Word has to say about it. So, before I can listen to what you have to say, I have some questions to ask you. First, I want to know if you agree with what Isaiah 55: 11 says?" (Have them read it out loud. When finished say) *** "This verse says that whatever God says will not return to Him unfulfilled, but His Word will be done. This leads me to another question and I would appreciate a simple yes or no answer. ***Do you believe, as I have heard, that Jehovah speaks His Word of truth only through the Watchtower Society? That it is God's spokesman?"

J.W.: "Yes" (Don't accept any other answer nicely.)

You: *** "My other question is, if it is true that The Watchtower Society has predicted Armageddon would occur several times and it hasn't happened yet, how do you explain Deuteronomy 18: 21, 22? Let's look this up just to make sure I have it right."

Have them read it out loud. If they bring up the prophecy/prediction theory, it will most likely be here. You can either get your pre-marked dictionary or simply tell them there is no difference and to look it up in their own dictionary to see for themselves. Either way, proceed to the next statement. Don't let them get going in their direction-you don't have time for it, you don't need it!

You: *** "I believe that these scriptures are the infallible, indisputable Words of God and they stand for all time. So, if I believe what is written in Isaiah and Deuteronomy, that the word that God has spoken will always come true, then I must believe that any word given by someone who claims to speak for God that does not come true, is not from God. Therefore, I can't accept your message. Believe me, I'm not trying to be rude, but I sincerely believe that perhaps you should carefully consider what these scriptures are saying not only to me but to us all. You'll have to excuse me now. I really don't have time to continue this discussion, but I am glad you stopped by."

As you can see, you have carried the same theme all the way through from beginning to end. All you have to do is keep the conversation flowing in the same direction as you want it to. You don't need to be unkind, but it may require being tough.

Most Challenging Defense

There is a lot of material in this section that needs to be absorbed. It is the foundation for the most challenging of Jehovah's Witnesses' doctrines. It has to be given in its entirety or none of it will make any sense. And you will have to have some sense of it or you cannot give a good defense against any of the doctrines derived from this information. Since the material is so comprehensive, I will give the entire Jehovah's Witness belief relating to believers, heaven, hell, the dead, and the resurrection. Then I will give the Christians' beliefs and doctrines in a numerical listing in order to systematically debunk the J.W.'s beliefs.

Jehovah's Witness Challenging Beliefs

The clearest way to start is by stating that the J.W.'s doctrines concerning believers are based on two classes of people. These two classes of people have different hopes of eternal life. Finally, the two classes of people have different resurrections. Nearly all of their fundamental beliefs are based on these two views of believers. In fact, they interpret, read, and teach the Bible in light of this belief system. Let me begin by identifying one of these two classes of people.

The 144,000

They believe that the foremost group is made up of 144,000 spirit-anointed believers. They base this on the references to this group in the book of Revelation. Since this number of believers are the only ones specifically mentioned as being with Christ in heaven, the early founders of the Society concluded that this was the total number of believers who would have a heavenly hope. They expanded this doctrine by choosing other scriptures they believed substantiated this stance, such as Luke 12:32 where Jesus refers to His disciples as a "little flock." There are several other additions to this belief that are *very important to know*.

One important aspect is that each of the 144,000 is chosen directly by Jehovah God. The Holy Spirit is bestowed exclusively upon the ones in this group-it is not indwelling but rests upon them. The first people to be chosen were the twelve apostles whom Jesus chose directly. However, the apostles did not receive the anointing of the Spirit until the day of Pentecost when it was also poured out on the total of 120 people in the upper room. It then expanded to include other believers who were in the first century up to the death of the last apostle. The primary mission of the entire 144,000 is to herald and spread the good news of God's kingdom.

False teachings and apostasy consequently ran rampant after the apostles' deaths, which resulted in few if any being chosen (anointed) from the first century until Jehovah "restored" His true religion through Charles Taze Russell in 1879. Then, the anointing began again. (It is significant to note that their teaching was that the 144,000 were completely sealed in the 1930s. However, the Watchtower's current official online website states that there are still 8,000 anointed still here on earth.)

The most crucial thing for everyone to know is that J.W.s believe that Jesus' teachings were directed *only to* and *for* this 144,000 group of followers. Therefore, the governing body of the Watchtower Society concluded long ago that the entire New Testament *was written by* members of this elite group *for* members of the group. So their conclusion was, and is, that the New Testament writers could speak of everyone having a spiritual anointing and a heavenly hope since every believer they spoke or wrote to were members of the 144,000. *(This is why it is almost impossible to use your version of the New Testament without knowing what they believe and how their Bible reads, in making a defense to a Jehovah's Witness that all believers in Christ Jesus have the hope of an eternal, spiritual life in heaven.)* So we see that the individual members of this group not only have a distinctive position and hope, but they also have a special resurrection.

Before the doctrine of the resurrection for the 144,000 can be described, you need to know the J.W.'s doctrine on the state of the dead in general. They do not believe in the immortality of man's soul or spirit. They believe that the spirit is the breath, life force, or emotional nature of man and that is all. Therefore, when a human dies, his breath leaves and then he is just plain dead. He or she has no conscious existence at all. He is just buried and awaits his call to resurrection. This is the state of everyone who has died, including the early members of the 144,000 class up to the year 1914. Remember to keep in mind that J.W.s believe that Jehovah set up His heavenly kingdom in that year.

As the apostles and the other anointed first century

Christians died, they waited in their graves until the call for their resurrection. According to Jehovah's Witnesses' belief, this initial call came in 1914. This is when they claim that Jehovah established His heavenly kingdom and instituted Jesus/Michael as king. Since Jesus is not to rule alone, but rather with the 144,000, he gave the call for those "who had died in Christ" up to that time to be resurrected to rule with Him in heaven. Thus, the dead ones of the chosen class were invisibly resurrected with a spirit body and joined Christ in the heavenly realm. Then as each person of the anointed class (one of the 144,000) died since 1914, that person was "changed in the twinkling of an eye" at the moment of death. That person then joins Christ and the other members of the chosen members in heaven. In conclusion, the 144,000 are the only chosen ones to be kings and priests with Jesus. But this leaves the question: Where do the millions of other Jehovah's Witnesses come in?

The Great Crowd

The Watchtower Society maintained that there was a total of 144,00 believers to be saved until the 1930's era. From 1879 until the mid-30s the principal work of preaching, teaching, writing, printing, and dispensing their material was done by members of the elite class. They recognized in the early decades of the twentieth century that they couldn't do all the worldwide work all alone. So they recruited outside people to help with delivering the literature. Suddenly, they received a "revelation" that other people had the possibility of being saved. They were the people who were their help-ers in the kingdom work during the last days. Thus, they identified their helpers as "the great crowd," which is directly mentioned after the call to seal the 144,000 in Revelation 7.

These workers, however, did not have the same hope that the 144,000 did. If members of the "great crowd" worked hard enough and were/are faithful, their reward would eventually be everlasting life on a paradise earth.

Since the Society received this "progressive revelation" regarding this other group, they determined that the Bible (primarily the New Testament), which was written for the 144,000 only, was also very important to the "great crowd." If it was the standard for the 144,000, then it is the standard for everybody else. So all the moral and spiritual exhortations to those with the "heavenly hope" were to be the example for those who had the earthly hope as well.

The idea of an eternal earthly life came from the scriptural passages that mention a new heaven and a new earth (Isaiah 65:17; 66:22; 2 Peter 3:13; Revelation 21:1). Their new "light" revealed that since the 144,000 were to be in a new heaven, which had been cleansed of all evil, then the New Earth, which is to be cleansed of all evil at Armageddon, has to be populated by someone—namely the "great crowd" of helpers who come through the tribulation and Armageddon alive. A significant factor in their belief is that Revelation 7:9 states that the "great crowd" who came out of the great tribulation is standing *before the throne*. They deduced that the crowd can't be heavenly since they are "before the throne"; therefore, they were not in the direct presence of God. Their conclusion is that these people were on earth with physical bodies. There is a whole set of "substantiating" scriptural foundations for this "earth" doctrine, which starts in Genesis.

First, God created a perfect earth that was to remain forever and, consequently, He created man to have everlasting life on it forever. If this was God's plan in the beginning, this was God's ultimate plan for all time. The Watchtower maintains that there is nothing wrong with the earth that sinful man hasn't done to it. This is only one example of their thoughts.

J.W.s also believe the "great crowd" will fulfill other works on earth that Jehovah has for them to do during the 1,000 year reign of Christ. They are to bury the dead and dispose of the rubble resulting from Armageddon. They are to teach the "truth" to the resurrected dead who are not of the heavenly calling. They will cultivate the earth, which will return to a paradise. They will either be with their existing family or they will get married, conceive, have children, and repopulate the earth. If they pass the final test of Satan at the end of the 1,000 years, this will continue until the earth is fully populated.

There will be people of all age groups who will enter into the new order. Each person, according to J.W.s, does not stay at this physical age in the new world system. If the person is ninety-nine years old, his or her body will gradually regenerate to around age thirty, since that is usually the peak of human fitness. On the other hand, a baby of two days old will mature to the age of thirty. Despite the rejuvenation or aging process, no one is guaranteed eternal life on earth until they prove faithful for the 1,000 years. Each person must also pass the test of temptation and faithfulness when Satan is released after the millennium. If you are deserving of eternal life, then each person will be gradually transformed into a state of physical perfection on a perfected earth. Besides these two groups we need to consider the resurrected dead.

The Dead and Resurrection

Jehovah's Witnesses believe that the billions of people who have died from the beginning of creation have been laying dormant without any conscious existence anywhere. All of these people, with the exception of the 144,000, will be resurrected during the millennium, but not all at the same time.

They believe that an unknown number of people will be resurrected in one hundred-year spans as a learning, training, and testing period. I have been questioned by some people if this time period is correct. Do I mean the 1,000 year rule of Christ? No, this is not a mistake. Each person resurrected upon the earth must first meet their one-hundred year test before he or she can finish out the 1,000 years. These people receive neither a purely physical nor spiritual body. No J.W. knows for certain what this body is to be like, but it is earth-bound, it is a non-gender being, and it cannot marry or have children. Each person who died without knowing the real truth of God's Word (any non-Witness) will have to be taught the truth. If a resurrected one proves rebellious or unteachable during this time, then God completely annihilates him on the spot. They call this an "everlasting cutting off," since it would not fit God's love and mercy to throw a person into a place of eternal fiery torment. Hence, there is no hell but the common grave. However, if a person is allowed to finish out the 1,000 years, he or she will also become a teacher of the next wave of resurrection bodies. Nevertheless, the resurrected dead will not be assured of or have attained eternal life until after Satan's release at the end of the 1,000 years-just like the Armageddon survivors.

This pretty well sums up all the things that Jehovah's Witnesses believe regarding the two classes of believers, their hopes, their eternal destinies, the new heaven and new earth, the resurrection, and hell. You may feel this is a really bizarre set of doctrines and wonder how anyone could believe such things. Someone would have to be completely stupid. Be careful. It has nothing to do with intelligence. There are people who are highly educated with master's and doctorate

degrees who have accepted this teaching. It only takes ignorance of the Bible, not having the Holy Spirit, and the subtle
but convincing methods J.W.s use to persuade someone that
these beliefs are true. So, we now need to find out specifically
why these doctrines are wrong.

Christian Beliefs

This will not only specify the doctrine, but will give the biblical reasons why J.W.s are wrong. So hold on, here it goes.

1. *There is only one class of believers.* The Bible doesn't say
   anywhere within its pages that there are two different
   classes of Christ's followers. Also, the Bible doesn't even
   remotely suggest that it was written by or for any special class of believer. In contrast, the Bible does say that
   all who believe in Jesus will be "heirs of the heavenly
   kingdom." Scriptural proof of this is found in James 2:5:
   "Listen, my beloved brethren: Has God not chosen the
   poor of this world to be rich in faith and *heirs of the kingdom which He promised to those who love* Him?"

   Paul also wrote in Romans 3:22 that there is no difference among believers: "…even the righteousness of God,
   *through faith in Jesus Christ, to all and on all who believe.
   For there is no difference.*" Jesus also shows that all who
   serve Him will be with Him as written in John 12:26: "If
   anyone serves Me, let him follow Me; and where I am,
   there My servant will be also. If anyone serves Me, him
   My Father will honor."

2. *There is only one eternal destiny for believers.* This is much
   like number one; however, it explicitly shows that believers will go to heaven and not as J.W.s believe that some
   go to heaven and some J.W. believers remain on earth.
   No stronger proof can be given than what Jesus said

Himself in John 12:26: "*If anyone serves Me, let him fol-low Me; and where I am, there My servant will be also.* If anyone serves Me, him My Father will honor."

Special Note: Please ask your minister what your denomination's belief is concerning the new heavens and earth. There are varying ideas regarding this belief. It is helpful to know what your belief is because it is a fundamental belief for Jehovah's Witnesses that it will endure as it is except it will return to an Edenic paradise. I don't want you to be unprepared in case this comes up in any of your discussions.

3. *Resurrection.* Contrary to the Witnesses' teaching, there is no second-chance salvation for the dead by being resurrected for a trial period of a 100 years. It is plainly stated in Hebrews 9:27, "And *as it is appointed for man to die once, but after this the judgment.*" In addition to this, the J.W.'s scriptural foundation for this doctrine is in Isaiah 65:20. It does not say anywhere in the passage that either the child or the unrighteous person was ever dead, let alone resurrected and given a trial period of time.

Revelation 20:5, 7, 11–13,15 debunks several of their resurrection doctrines: Verse 5 states: "But the rest of the dead did not live again until the thousand years were finished…" proving that the resurrection of all, except believers in Christ, was not until after the 1,000 year reign. Thus, no one is resurrected during the 1,000 years. Verse 7 states: "Now when the thousand years have expired…," also proving that Christ's thousand-year reign has already ended before the resurrection takes place. Verse 11, 12 states: "Then I saw a great white throne and Him who sat on it, from whose face the earth and the heaven fled away. And there was found no place for them. And I saw the dead, small and great, standing before God, and books were opened. And another book was opened, which is the Book of Life. And the dead were judged according to their works, by the things which were written in the books." This clearly proves that God passes judgment on all the resurrected dead just once after the 1,000 years.

Verse 13 states: "The sea gave up the dead who were in it, and Death and Hades delivered up the dead who were in them. And they were judged, each one according to his works." This proves that all the dead are resurrected at one time and not in any specific or multiple time periods, such as one hundred years. The wording of this verse also proves that the dead were judged only once at the end of the 1,000 years.

Verse 15 states: "And anyone not found written in the Book of Life was cast into the lake of fire." This clearly shows once again that judgment and punishment is meted out to the resurrected dead at this time.

4. *Hell-Fire Punishment for Wicked.* J.W.'s belief that the wicked are punished by "everlasting cutting off" or permanent death is dashed to pieces by Hebrews 10:28, 29: "Anyone who has rejected Moses' law dies without mercy on the testimony of two or three witnesses. Of how much worse punishment, do you suppose, will he be thought worthy who has trampled the Son of God underfoot, counted the blood of the covenant by which he was sanctified a common thing, and insulted the Spirit of grace?"

And here is also something else to think about. Hebrews 10:31 says, "It is a fearful thing to fall into the hands of the living God." God could kill a person in a fraction of a second, which would hold little or no pain. What kind of punishment would that be? In keeping with eternal punishment, the fire is eternal and never goes out (Mark 9:43; Revelation 14:11).

The Watchtower's doctrine of complete annihilation also does not agree with the Bible. It clearly shows that there are varying degrees of punishment, such as being cutting in two (Matthew 24:51), being put in with the unbelievers (Luke 12:46), and beaten with many or few stripes (Luke 12:47–48). This is not to say exactly what judgment is meted out on any particular person, but it does show that not everyone has the same punishment. Now, how can you use all of this to make a defense?

Special Note: Please also investigate what your denomination believes regarding the lake of fire and the second death mentioned in Revelations 20:14. There are also varying beliefs regarding this passage. I believe this way (put simply): the first death was physical death, the second death is spiritual death since no reconciliation with God is possible after the great white throne judgment has taken place. This does not however mean that there is not any punishment/suffering incurred by unbelievers via God's judgment. However, it is important to know what you believe since this also is a principal doctrine of J.W.s.

Most Challenging Defenses

This section is different than the preceding ones. If you have made it this far, you will be able to put together your own methods of defense. The current format will be to give a topic, the scriptures from the New King James Version that can be used with the New World Translation, and relative questions or statements that provoke thought or make the point. I will not, however, give full scripture citations from this point on. You have learned from previous examples that the translations are similar in content. I must stress that you should have learned not only the information on J.W.'s beliefs in this section, but most of the information throughout. Especially if you want to give a good, thorough witness to them.

Here are some notes of caution. Remember all of these topics are Jehovah's Witness' foundational doctrines. They will try their best to turn the encounter into their witness. Do not let them do it. If they start, just kindly interrupt them and bring them back to the points you want to make with the scriptures you want to use.

One Class of Believers

- *Purpose:* To show that there is no difference between believers.
- *Recommended Scriptures:* Romans 3:22; James 2:5; John 12:26.
- *Question to ask:* *** " Is it true that you believe that only 144,00 people go to heaven? Just a yes or no will do. (After their answer.) I need to tell you that I believe something different."
- *Foundation Statement:* *** "I believe that all believers go to heaven because of what the Bible says at Romans 3:22." (Reference to no difference among believers. Have them read it.) "I also believe it because of Jesus' promises. Would you look up James 2:5?" (All who love Jesus will be heirs.) "Now would you look up John 12: 26?" (Those who follow Jesus and serve/minister for Him will be with Him. *** Note: their Bible has minister instead of serve.)
- *Statement:* *** " I love Jesus. I also follow, serve, and minister for Jesus. Based on these scriptures, that means that I and everyone else who puts Jesus first will go to heaven."

- *Accomplished:* What you have done is used exactly what they say their main mission, which is to preach the Gospel because they love, follow, and serve Jehovah. The emphatic point should be that Christians must follow and serve *Jesus*.

Hell

- *Purpose:* to show that people do not just die. To show there is conscious existence after death and the wicked are cast into an eternal place of punishment. To show that there are degrees of punishment.
- *Recommended Scriptures:* Hebrews 10:29; Revelation 14:11.
- *Initial Statement/Question:* *** "I've heard that J.W.s do not believe there is a real place of hell-fire in which the wicked are punished. Yes or no, is that true?" (You have to be careful how you phrase this question. If you just ask them if they believe in hell, they will answer yes. They believe it is the common grave.)
- *Statement:* "Do you have time for me to tell you why I believe that death is not all there is? Would you look up Hebrews 10:29? ***See, it says that people under Moses' Law merely suffered death for disobedience and unbelief, but for people who reject Christ there is a much worse punishment. In fact, I believe that sinners will be punished forever and ever. I also believe this is what the Bible teaches in Revelation 14:11. Now that says that the smoke of sinners' rises forever and ever. The Bible also tells us that sinners don't even suffer the

same judgment." (You can use any of these scriptures: Luke 12:46–48; Matthew 10:15, 21–24; or Revelation 20:13. Then make the point you want to and conclude.)

Resurrection

- *Purpose:* To show that there is no "second chance" for salvation. To show that all of the resurrected dead rise and receive the judgment of reward or punishment at the same time.
- *Recommended Scriptures:* Hebrews 9:27; Revelation 20:5, 7, 13, 15.
- *Question:* *** "Is it true that you believe that the dead are not resurrected all at one time, but every 100 years during the 1,000 year Reign of Christ? I have limited time so could you please give me a yes or no answer?"
- *Initial Statement:* *** " I have to base what I believe on the Bible, and I believe what Hebrews 9: 27 says." (After it's read) "See, it says that man only dies once then the judgment. I also don't understand about the 1,000 years of resurrection because the Bible says Christ's 1,000 year reign is over before the judgment takes place. I believe I have it right, but why don't you look up Revelation 20:5, 7, 13, and 15, and let's see for sure." (After it's read.) *** "Now, you must agree that these verses tell us that the final resurrection doesn't take place until the 1,000 years have already ended. That the dead are all judged at the same time. It also doesn't say that they are in any way put to death again."

You may conclude with your stance that you will go with the Bible's truth.

If you feel comfortable and confident, you could ask them how the 100-year resurrection takes place. They will direct you to Isaiah 65:20: "No more will there come to be a suckling a few days old from that place, neither an old man that does not fulfill his days; for one will die as a mere boy, although a hundred years of age; and as for the sinner, although a hundred years of age he will have evil called down upon him" (NWT). You can still remain solid by stating that nowhere does that verse show that anyone had died or been resurrected.

Although I have given some solid grounds to work on, it is entirely your choice how you use the material that has been presented. It is possible to incorporate different topics and methods into one encounter. It typically depends on what your biblical knowledge is to begin with and how easily the needed information regarding J.W.s can be digested. As has been stated throughout, the hope is that it will result in a peaceable, effective witness for the Gospel in whatever path you take.

Conclusion

My overall hopes have been that this book will be a book of truth and understanding. Truth by fully realizing what God wants for all men, life. I feel that the only way we can do this is by recognizing that Satan and all his forces of darkness with their goals of deception, lies, and death are the ones behind the cults', Jehovah's Witnesses', beliefs.

It is only by recognizing these two opposing goals that perhaps we can finally see why J.W.s find the Watchtower Society's messages so appealing: Satan's deceiving doctrines and methods have led people into accepting his lies disguised as God's truth. We can also discover why and how people get involved with that organization. We may be able to better understand why their minds have been so clouded that it has resulted in their rejection of our efforts at Christian evangelism. The bottom line is that maybe we can perceive them as ordinary people who need to be set free from the bondage of darkness and fear.

It is only by this understanding, as I feel the Lord has given His word to me, that we can break free from the biases, misunderstandings, and mysteries that surround J.W.s. Only then can we be most effective for God by speaking His word of life and ultimately defeating Satan and the forces of darkness in peoples' lives.

A fitting conclusion, now that it has all been said and done, is to share with you what my prayer has been for each of us regarding this book

> Dear God of heaven and earth, You are the Creator of all things. I praise You and thank You for the opportunity to serve You. I have tried to do what Your purpose has been for me, and to speak Your words in Your way and at Your Time, not mine. I pray that each person who reads this will seek Your face to find what you have for them to do and how You want them to do it. Dear Father, only You know what each one needs. I pray that You open their hearts and eyes to know Your love, plan, and desire You have for all people. Open their hearts to change. Open their eyes of understanding so the light of Your love and word will shine forth into the spiritual darkness that envelops Jehovah's Witnesses. I also ask that You strengthen their faith and increase their knowledge in love. O, Holy Father, I pray for You to give each one the boldness to speak the Word. Jesus is the Word, and He is living in us all. Help us to let that Word bubble forth into a fountain of life wherever we may go. Father, You know who will sow a seed, let it find fertile ground. You know who will water that seed, let the Holy Spirit supply the rain and sun. You know who will cultivate it, Lord, breathe life into it. You know who will harvest where others have worked, let the harvest be fine fruit. Gracious Father, thank You. I love You and give You

all the glory and praise, through Your Son and our
King and Redeemer, Jesus the Christ of Nazareth,
and by the Holy Spirit. Amen, Amen, and Amen.

Reference guide
for believers

Jesus

As God:	John 1:1; 8: 58; 10:30; 20:28 Colossians. 1: 15- 16; 2:9 Titus 2:13 Hebrews 1:8
All knowing:	Matthew 11:27; 17: 27 Luke 5:4,6 John 7: 29; 8: 55; 10:15; 16:30; 17:25; 21:17; 21:6–11
Chose to be unknow- ing as human:	Philippians 2:5–11 Mark: 13:32
Worshiped:	Matthew 2: 11; 8: 2 9:18; 28:9; 28:17 John 9:38 John 20: 28

Holy Spirit
He's a Person:

Has a mind:	Romans 8:27
Has a will:	1 Corinthians 12: 11
Has emotion:	Ephesians 4: 30

His Abilities

Teaches:	John 14: 26
Testifies:	John15:26
Guides:	Romans 8:14
Commands:	Acts 8:29
Speaks:	John15:26; 2 Peter 1:21

Is God

Qualities of:	Psalm139:7 1 Corinthians 2:10 Romans 15:9 John16:7–14 Hebrews 9:14
Works of:	Genesis 1:2 Psalm104:30 2 Peter 1:21 Titus 3:5

One Class of Believers

All believers are "heirs in heavenly kingdom:"	Galatians 3: 29; 4:28–31 Titus3:7 James2:5
All believers in Christ have heavenly destiny:	Ephesians 2: 19 Philippians 3:20 Colossians 3:1 Hebrews 3:1; 12:22 2 Peter 1:10–11
No difference in believers:	Romans 3:22
All servants/ministers will be with Jesus:	John 12:26
All believers are one flock with one shepherd:	John 10:16

Hell

Real place of suffering:	Matthew 5:22; 18:8; 25:41 Jude 7 Revelation 22:14
Eternal and unquenchable:	Mark 9: 43 Revelation 14: 11
Degrees of punishment:	Matthew 10: 15; 11: 21–24 Luke 12: 47–48 John 15: 22 Hebrews 19:29 Revelation 20:11–15 Revelation 22:12

ruth baker

Scriptures compatible with NWT

Jesus

Jesus is God:	John 20:28
Jesus and God both called Alpha and Omega:	Revelation1: 8 Revelation 22:12,13
Jesus and God both shown to send angel:	Revelation 2: 6 Revelation 22:16

Holy Spirit

Holy Spirit is a person/being:	John13, 14; Acts10:19, 20 Acts 13:2
Holy Spirit is God:	Acts 5:3

Believers go to Heaven

Jesus Promises that those who follow, serve/minister will be w/ Him:	John 12:26
No Difference between believers w/faith:	Romans 3: 22
Jesus promised those who love Him to be heirs with Him:	James 2: 5

There is Hell-Fire Punishment

Fire is eternal and unquenchable:	Mark 9:43 Revelation 14:11
There are degrees of punishment/not ever-lasting cutting-off:	Luke 12: 46–48 Matthew 10:15; 24:51 Revelation 20:11–13
Wicked's punish-ment not just death:	Hebrews 10:29 Revelation 14:11

Resurrection

Man only dies and is judged once:	Hebrews 9: 27
Occurs after the 1,000 reign of Christ:	Revelation 20:5, 7
Everyone in the last resur-rection rises at same time:	Revelation 20: 13
Judgment to punish-ment also after 1,000 years completed:	Revelation 20: 15

False Prophets

Prophet who speaks for God must come true:	Deuteronomy 18:21, 22
God's Word always fulfilled:	Isaiah 55: 11
There are present day false teachers and prophets:	2 Peter 2: 1